Hoping for a Happy Ending

*A journalist's story of depression,
bipolar and alcoholism*

Christine Stapleton

authorHOUSE®

AuthorHouse™
1663 Liberty Drive
Bloomington, IN 47403
www.authorhouse.com
Phone: 1-800-839-8640

First published by AuthorHouse 8/28/2009

ISBN: 978-1-4389-9150-4 (sc)
ISBN: 978-1-4389-9151-1 (hc)
ISBN: 978-1-4389-9152-8 (e)

Editor's Note: The columns that appear in this book were first published
in The Palm Beach Post, which granted the author permission to
republish them. Cover art is a cloud tag of Searching for a happy ending
created by www.wordle.net. Back cover photo by Ray Graham.

Printed in the United States of America
Bloomington, Indiana

This book is printed on acid-free paper.

Dedication
To my Father,
Mom, Dad, Marsha & John
Dog
And the love of my life
Kealy Megan

Acknowledgments

I am blessed to have a very long gratitude list. Without these people there would be a large hole in my soul.

Nicole Neal and Carolyn Dipaolo, my brilliant editors at The Palm Beach Post

The girlfriends: You know who you are. I love you all

Pam, my guardian angel

Dana, my therapist

Pat, my nurse practitioner

Bill W. and Dr. Bob.

Introduction

This book is the byproduct of what originally seemed like a really bad idea. Several months after my diagnosis and recovery from a major clinical depression in 2006, my therapist suggested I write about my experience. "No way," I told her. "Absolutely no way."

But as I returned to my regularly scheduled life I realized that nothing was – or ever would be – the same. I recognized that my recovery had not occurred in a vacuum. I had not done it alone. Recovery from mental illness is a "We" program. I wanted to share what had been so freely given to me.

With the consent of the editors at The Palm Beach Post I began writing a weekly column on mental illness called "Kicking Depression." This book is a compilation of selected columns and entries from my blog *Depression on My Mind* at PsychCentral.com. *Hoping for a Happy Ending* is the story that launched my column and explains how I found, fell into and crawled out of my black hole.

I hope these writings help you as much as they have helped me. We are all in this together.

Hoping for a happy ending

Years ago I bought a poster of Rosie the Riveter, framed it and hung it above the desk where I write on my front porch. I love Rosie. She is the face of millions of women who rolled up their sleeves and headed to the steel mills, shipyards and factories during World War II.

Rosie nixed the notion that brawn and beauty were incompatible and that women weren't capable of handling a job and a home. Her nails are polished. Her mascara is perfect. Her right arm flexed as she rolls her work shirt over her bicep. A perfectly plucked left eyebrow is raised just enough to say We Can Do It!

Rosie is my hero. She is strong. She is beautiful. She is me.

I believed this until April 25, 2006. On that day everything I thought I knew about myself shattered. The image of the capable woman so many people had of me - award-winning journalist, single mom, bread winner and baker - sat sobbing on a park bench at 5 a.m. as my puzzled dog watched. I had begun a journey into a hell I did not know existed. A hole so deep and black, I could only focus on ending it. A hell called depression.

I was scared. I was alone. I was human.

I was not Rosie.

I thought I knew about depression. I have friends who have been depressed. I would tell them how badly I felt for them and ask if I could help. Privately I thought, come on, get a grip. Eat some chocolate. Walk on the beach. Put peanut butter on your dog's nose. Go rent *Caddyshack*, for Chrissake. Lord knows I have known sadness and grief. Death, divorce, illness. But depression - a real major clinical depression - is much, much more than being really, really sad.

Although it is no consolation to those of us who have this disease, we are not alone. There are about 21 million Americans who suffer from depression every year. It is the leading cause of disability in the United States. The economic toll is $83 billion annually.

King David and Job had it. So did Goethe, Tolstoy and Florence Nightingale. Actor Drew Carey. Journalist Mike Wallace. Even the Beaver's brother, Wally Cleaver, had it. It killed Kurt Cobain. Winston Churchill named his depression his "black dog." I call mine my "black hole."

My depression is cunning and baffling. It tries to convince me that I am not sick. It tells me that I'm just not trying hard enough. I am a loser. I am a selfish ingrate. Depression tells me to pull myself up by my bootstraps. Keep trying. I can think my way out of this mess. Look at all I have. I should be happy.

And I should be happy. Hell, I should be ecstatic. I have a wonderful life. My 14-year-old daughter and I have traveled the world. She loves school, has great friends and gets good grades. Her college is already paid for. I have a beautiful home in a trendy neighborhood. I have wonderful friends. I have money in the bank. I can still wear a bikini.

So why was I sitting on a park bench at 5 a.m. on April 25 wondering how long it would take to kill myself - or if I even could - with a hose hooked up to the exhaust of my Toyota Prius, a hybrid that has almost no lethal emissions?

In hindsight, my depression makes perfect sense. On that day there was a perfect confluence of genetics, grief and chemical imbalance in my brain. I fell into a black hole. I could not get out. I could not hit bottom. I just fell deeper and deeper and deeper.

That day is a blur. I woke up crying. I finally made it to work and as I walked by the security desk I had a feeling that I was not in my body. Someone asked me a question. I couldn't answer. I left. I called a psychiatrist's office. They offered me an appointment the following week. I remember saying: "I need to see someone now."

The nurse asked a lot of questions. Yes, I had thought about suicide. Yes, I had tried to kill myself before, as a teenager. No, I wasn't going to do it. I love my daughter too much and could never leave her. They gave me medicine. I took it. I don't remember the rest of that day, or the next, or the next. They are all a blur.

I remember trying to watch television. It sounded tinny and hurt my ears. The story line of an episode of *Law & Order* seemed impossibly complex. The memory of an article I had read only moments ago vanished. I bounced between inconsolable and catatonic. I could not focus on the newspaper that had published my stories for nearly 20 years.

People who know me - co-workers and friends - will tell you that I am a strong woman. I have run marathons, triathlons and ridden 100-mile bike races. I scuba dive. I ski. I mountain bike. I volunteer. I restored my 80-year-old home. I go to the gym before the sun rises. I read the Bible at breakfast.

How could this be happening to me?

Had I known more about depression I would have known that I had suffered with depression since I was a child and had grown up with a mild state of depression called dysthemia. I would have understood that nothing I achieved - the trophies, the scholarship, the byline - could ever have made me happy.

I would have known that this disease runs in my family and all my gold stars, blue ribbons or a million Hail Mary's could never have made my depressed mother happy.

I would have known that the endorphin rush I got running back and forth across the Blue Heron bridge until my heart rate reached 180 beats per minute was just a desperate attempt to self-medicate myself.

I would have known about "situational depression" - a type of depression caused by a loss - and that a steady stream of devastating losses in my life and my reluctance and inability to grieve them had exacerbated my chronic depression.

I would have known I was a major clinical depression waiting to happen.

My 10-year marriage had ended in May 1999 and left me a full-time single working mother. My daughter was 6. By February 2001 I was in the hospital with pneumonia, exhausted from working countless hours on the newspaper's coverage of the November 2000 election. Eight months later my father died of lung cancer. Five days after his funeral my mother began another round of chemotherapy. Her colon cancer had spread to her liver.

On March 6, 2003 - 16 months after my father's death - my mother died a slow, painful death that robbed her of her dignity. By the end of the summer our family's home for 35 years - the kitchen where Mom canned applesauce, the bedroom heating duct where I hid my diary, the basement where we listened to Led Zeppelin - was gone. Sold to a young family.

Without my mother - the glue that held our family together - my brother and sister and I became estranged. We talked only on holidays and birthdays. I felt like an orphan. Nine months later my beloved dog

Bella died in my arms. She was 14. It was cancer. I buried her in the back yard.

Reeling like a stubborn boxer on the mat, I got back on my feet and plunged back into my life. I assumed grief was like a sad movie that ended with the last spade of dirt thrown on a grave. I was wrong. Very wrong. One more loss finally pushed me into my black hole.

I had fallen in love with a man in the spring of 2000. Six years of juggling a career, terminally ill parents and single parenting had strained our relationship. I wanted couples' counseling. He wanted out and declared our six-year relationship over. Ten weeks later he had a new girlfriend. She was "available," he said. Her children were grown. He took her to Las Vegas.

I was crushed. I had tried dating but my heart wasn't in it. I couldn't sleep. I lost 20 pounds. My chest was tight and my heart raced. My doctor ordered a stress test. My heart was fine. I was stressed. I started therapy and got on my knees every night and begged God not to take the only love left in my life - my daughter.

My therapist and my girlfriends told me I needed help. I needed to consider antidepressants. I balked. I can handle this, I thought. Look at all I've been through. Time heals all wounds, right? Then I learned it's not time that heals the wounds. It's what you do while time passes that heals the wounds.

A friend of mine, a respected physician, admitted taking antidepressants. Many of my friends - strong, successful career women - admitted that they were on antidepressants. I was shocked and saddened that so many of my friends not only suffered from depression but had felt too ashamed to discuss it. I agreed to take antidepressants.

My experience with prescription drugs is nearly nil - the occasional antibiotic and Novocain at the dentist, drugs that work fast. Antidepressants, I learned from the psychiatric nurse treating me, can take up to six weeks to reach their full effect. And they might not work at all, she said. And they might make my depression worse, she added.

Three weeks later I felt no better. One of my medications was increased. I became more depressed. Another medication was added to my regime. Within a week I was beginning to feel better. However, drugs would not be enough to manage this disease, she said.

I needed to continue my therapy, exercise, eat even if I wasn't hungry to stabilize my blood sugar, keep a journal about my feelings and deal with my anger.

Anger? What anger? I had never considered myself an angry person. I didn't understand. For many women, depression is anger turned inward, she explained. And anger is a healthy emotion and a necessary phase of grief, my therapist said.

I had never been given permission to be angry. As a child, anger was not an acceptable emotion. Growing up I learned anger wasn't lady-like. But now my therapist wanted me to beat a pillow with a whiffle bat. Scream. Shout. Get mad. Get it out. Suddenly I realized I wasn't angry. I didn't have whiffle-bat anger. I had junkyard rage. I wanted to break something. I wanted to hear my rage. I wanted to do damage.

I got myself a metal bat. I pulled out the Yellow Pages and found a junk yard. I put on the steel-toed boots I had bought after one of the hurricanes, found the pair of gloves my daughter had used at sailing camp years ago and crammed a Rolling Stones CD into my car's stereo.

It was a raining when I pulled into the junkyard's muddy parking lot. I walked to the office and explained my predicament to the guys behind the counter. "They say I need to do this to feel better," I explained. The guys didn't blink.

"You want a bat or a golf club," one guy said pointing to a pile of bats and golf clubs in the corner.

"I have my own bat," I said. "It's metal." He smiled.

"Are you gonna scream?" he asked.

"I don't know," I said.

We walked past wrecked cars stacked on top of each other. Then he pointed to the frame of a green truck. Some of the windows were gone but the grill, headlights and driver's window were intact, along with the hood and front quarter-panels.

He pointed: "You can hit this truck, but only this one." Then he walked away.

I started with the hood, moved on to the grill, took out both headlights, the driver's window and the right front quarter-panel before I stopped, completely exhausted. I have no idea how long I was there. I went back to the office and asked if they wanted me to clean up my mess.

"Nope," the guy said, giving me a look I had never seen on a man's face before. Utter respect.

"Thanks," I said and walked back to the car, dragging my bat. My hands were shaking but I felt good. Really good. Better than I had felt in weeks.

I decided then that I will attack this disease. I will do what the doctor and therapist tell me. I will take my medications no matter how good I feel. I will learn to say "no" when I feel overwhelmed. I will cry when I am sad. I will learn to get mad without a bat. I will not be ashamed to tell people that I have depression.

I will get better.

It's depression - not a character defect

I don't exactly know how to say it.
"I was depressed."
"I was in a major clinical depression."
"I was diagnosed with depression."
"I have depression."

What's the best way to explain why you were off work for two months? Why you couldn't make it to your kid's ballgame? Why you haven't washed your hair in a week? Why you lost/gained 20 pounds?

At some time everyone says "I'm depressed." They mean they're sad, feeling blue. They don't mean that they are slit-your-wrists, toaster-in-the-tub, jump-off-the-roof depressed. They're just unhappy. And I don't want to confuse my depression with someone's bad hair day.

I don't want this disease to define me, either. Would someone with cancer say "I am cancered?" No. So, why should I say "I am depressed?" I am not this disease. Some people have cancer. Some people have depression. I choose to say: "I have depression."

If you don't have depression this little semantic exercise probably sounds ridiculous. Who gives a hoot?

We do. People with depression care. We care because we want you to stop treating depression like it is a character defect. We care because we want you to treat us with the same compassion and understanding that you would give to someone whose body can't produce and process certain other chemicals - such as insulin.

We want you to stop treating us like we're lazy ingrates. We want to be able to admit that we have a disease and that we want and need help.

I can think of only one other physical condition that affects so many but is so taboo: erectile dysfunction. An estimated 15 million to 40 million American men suffer from erectile dysfunction. But do you know of one, besides Bob Dole and Rush Limbaugh? I don't.

I'm not saying I want to open a dialogue about the male genitalia. However, I would like for people with depression to feel as comfortable talking about their disease as women with breast cancer feel to freely discuss their breasts.

This may sound extreme. But consider this: There are countless meetings everyday for alcoholics to discuss their disease. Every year thousands support breast cancer research by running the Race for the Cure. Sports legends play celebrity golf tournaments to raise money for juvenile diabetes.

An estimated 14 million Americans suffer a major episode of depression every year. Millions more struggle daily with mild forms of depression. How about a charity ball for us? How about we raise a pile of money for treatment for the uninsured who suffer from this disease and can't get the therapy or medications they need?

There are a few depression support groups out there and they do wonderful work. Still, nobody really wants to talk about mental illness or admit they are mentally ill. I hadn't realized this until I started telling my friends that I have depression. I was shocked and saddened to learn many of my girlfriends - strong, capable women that I have known for years - admitted that they, too, were on antidepressants. I never knew.

I mean, if we don't feel comfortable telling our best friends that we have this disease, who can we tell?

Sometimes, trying to help doesn't help

There are some things you just don't say to someone in a major depression. My favorite, the one that really grinds me, is: "Look how much you have to be grateful for . . ."

My brother-in-law said this to me during a phone call. I know he meant well. He was only trying to help. Then he rattled off the wonderful things in my life: My daughter is healthy; I have a good job, a great little house, money in the bank . . .

Stop.

Like I don't know this? Of course I know this! When I'm standing on the edge of my "black hole," just before I fall in, I play that ingrate tape in my brain. Over and over. It sounds like this: "How can I feel horrible when I have all these things, all these people who care for me? Snap out of it! You think you have it bad? Look how bad so-and-so has it. You are such a loser. You don't deserve to have such a good life. There are women in (name your favorite country of strife) who watch their children starve. Their daughters are raped by soldiers. Their husbands are kidnapped in the middle of the night. . . . And you, you spend your weekends walking the beach."

You get the picture.

Believe me. At a certain point in depression, we beat ourselves up over the fact we can't pull ourselves out of it. You don't have to remind us of what we have. And when you do remind us, it only makes us feel worse.

My other favorite is: "Wow, you always seemed to have your life so together."

OK. Why does having depression mean I don't have my life together? Would you say that to someone whose body can't regulate sugar? Most of the time I do have my life together. I go to work every day, I cook healthy meals, I exercise, I walk the dog, I pay the bills. Just like you. But sometimes my brain doesn't produce and process the chemicals it needs to be healthy. I get depressed and I can't do these things. Just like someone who has chronic back problems and sometimes can't mow the lawn, vacuum or empty the dishwasher.

Then there are the "You shoulds."

Here are my favorites. "You should": keep busy; try yoga; exercise; try coconut oil; journal; get out more; rent a funny movie; take antidepressants; don't take antidepressants; pray; go shopping; go to church; meditate; eat chocolate; drink herbal tea; take a bath; keep a journal; read a good book.

I know you are trying to help but enough.

What I want is for you to listen. Just listen. Pretend you are a big ear or a bobble-head doll. You don't have to say anything. Just be with me.

Let me ramble. Let me stare. Let me cry. Let me know that even though you can't understand what I am going through, you will be there. Just let me know that I'm not alone in the black hole. Let me know that you will not judge me for the way I act when this disease strikes.

That's all.

A good night's rest, by George

I never had good dreams. At least I never remember having a good dream. In my dreams the anxiety and stress of the day lived on in weird dramas with real-life characters miscast in bizarre roles. In some dreams I could fly but inevitably I looked down and panicked when I realized I had no idea how to land. Or I would lose my daughter in a market in London that looked conspicuously like the McDonald's near the World Trade Center in New York.

Even though I couldn't remember most of my dreams, they set my mood for the day. I would wake up with a rotten tightness in my chest. Tired, feeling lonely, anxious, sad and hopeless. I figured this was normal. Just my brain trying to work out some emotional kinks.

And I was tired. So tired. Sleep was like chocolate. I could never get enough. Even if I managed to get to bed early, I would invariably wake up at 3 a.m. - my mind racing, my chest tight worrying about whether I would be able to find someone to help me with my hurricane shutters this year.

So it was such a relief when the psychiatric nurse practitioner who monitors my medications, looked at me - a catatonic, red-eyed zombie who had walked into her office a suicidal wreck - and uttered these words: "First, we need to get you some sleep."

What did sleep have to do with depression? Everything, I learned. The lack of good, sound sleep was fueling the chemical imbalance in my brain, she said. Sleep was my first assignment in dealing with my depression. The antidepressants could take weeks to kick in, the nurse practitioner explained. Sound sleep was what I needed immediately, she said.

I don't like to take drugs. But my desire for a good night's sleep and my utter defeat in the face of my depression convinced me that the nurse practitioner knew what she was doing and that she was right. I agreed to take a pill to help me sleep.

Thirty minutes after taking the pill I lay down in bed. One thought - only one thought - crawled through my mind, not a million racing around, bouncing off the inside of my cranium. This is nice, I thought. One thought at a time. What a concept.

I slept for 12 hours. I could barely wake up. Even caffeine didn't help. I went back to bed and slept through the afternoon.

Two weeks later, my body was rested and the sluggishness was gone.

And then it happened: The George Clooney Dream.

Never has there been a dream like this. At least not in my head. That night began like any other night. I took my meds, said my prayers and drifted off.

At 5 a.m., I awoke. Smiling. I had had a dream that George Clooney was madly in love with me, couldn't keep his hands off me and wanted to marry me. Seriously. I couldn't believe it. A good dream. A really good dream. So good I tried to fall back asleep and slide back into the part about George not being able to keep his hands off me.

Unfortunately, I was too excited to sleep. A good dream! It was too early to call my friends so I sent them e-mails, explaining the Clooney epiphany.

Later that week I went to see the nurse practitioner. She asked how I was doing on my meds. I told her about The George Clooney Dream. She smiled. "That's the serotonin kicking in," she said. I told her I had never had good dreams.

She assured me I would have more. But she couldn't guarantee George would be in them.

Going public – or not

What do I say at work? What do I tell my co-workers? How do I explain my sudden departure and the two months away from the newsroom?

These were my biggest fears about coming back to work after the eight-week medical leave I took when I slipped into a major clinical depression in April. My bosses had faithfully abided by privacy laws that prevented them from explaining my absence to my co-workers.

So, it was up to me. I got to decide what to say. Or not to say.

This was a huge dilemma for me. For more than 20 years, I have made a living asking people extremely personal questions. When I'm on a story, I plow through court files, police reports, job applications and depositions looking for personal details. I call neighbors, exes, former teachers and bosses, looking for comments. It's part of my job.

But now it was my turn. I was in the hot seat. When you work in a newsroom filled with people who are trained to ask probing questions, you have to be prepared.

I asked my friends what they would do.

"Remember what happened to Jane Pauley?" one girlfriend said. "God, you don't want to go public. Look what they did to her."

"What about your career?" another friend asked. "If they know that you have depression, you'll never get promoted. They will never put you on another big, breaking story."

I worried about the snide comments I had heard in the newsroom about mental illness. I shook my head at the wisecracks but never said anything. Now the joke was on me.

My therapist left it up to me. My psychiatric nurse practitioner agreed. Both were adamant. Depression is a disease. It is not a character defect. It is not my fault. I am not a weak person. I have an illness.

Their warnings were just as direct - mentally ill people are stigmatized. There will be people who will consider you less capable, who will consider you just another woman who had a "mental breakdown." You will be lumped into that mass of medicated Americans who Tom Cruise criticized - the folks who reach for a happy pill and listen to psychobabble when they feel blue.

Or, I could just lay it all on the table. Explain to anyone who asked that I have depression. Be completely honest.

I realized that I had gotten to a point in my life where the things that had seemed so important when I was building my career, my bank account and my family, just weren't important anymore. I realized that what others think of me didn't matter. It's what I think of myself. The skeletons I had been hiding were just dried bones. Keeping secrets is just too much work.

I have no husband. My parents are dead. My depression proved to me that I have incredibly loyal friends who don't care what kind of car I drive or shoes I wear. My teenage daughter is wise beyond her years and will always be there for me.

So I decided to "out" myself.

I have depression.

There. No big deal. I'm back.

Depression: In the beginning

It starts like this: the muscles in my face, just below my eyes and around my mouth, go completely slack. The top and back of my eyeballs ache and an exhausting dull pressure deposits itself on each temple. I am tired. Very, very tired. I just want to curl up in a fetal position in my bed, under my covers, and sleep. But life goes on. I have stuff to do. So, I do the stuff I have to do, with my long face and empty eyes.

Sometimes I just stare. If you asked, I would have to really think what time and day it is. I want to be alone - except for my dog. I am sliding and I know it. I wake up and tell myself this is going to be a good day. And it is, for a couple hours. Then I start sliding. Sometimes I run home at lunch for a nap. I drink coffee and Diet Pepsi to stay awake. I don't look at people when I talk to them. I look past them.

Wednesday my editor called me into her office. She knows my illnesses and me. She gets it. Several years ago, upon returning from a two month leave after a deep depression, I asked her to spot me. Keep an eye on me. Reel me in when you first see me start to slide. Please.

"You asked me to let you know. You are flat," she said. "I see you're having trouble focusing." Gently, she asked me to call my doctor. I reluctantly agree.

"Today?" she asked.

"Yes," I sighed. "I hate this."

"Why? Because it means you're not perfect?" she asked - not sarcastic but genuinely concerned.

"No," I told her. "If there is one thing I know it is that I am not perfect." I have two divorces and a string of bad relationships to prove it.

"I just hate this," I explained. I hate having depression and bipolar. I hate that every time something bad happens to me, I can't seem to control myself and my emotions like other people. I hate that I get so sad and scared. I hate that voice I hear in my head that says, "Oh, she committed suicide." I hate raging against that voice and screaming back - with every fiber in my being - "NOOOOOOOOO!" in my head. Suicide is never - ever - an option.

I can get through this. I will get through this. I always come out the other side. I am OK. I have done nothing wrong. I am a good person. I am just sick. And I will try very, very hard to get well and stay well. I am not a quitter. This is about chemicals and hormones.

So, I called my psych-nurse practitioner and my therapist. My nurse adjusted my meds. It will take a couple of weeks before I know if the new dosage works. Then I met with my therapist - until 8 p.m. I need to remember that I am in charge of what I think. I do not have to obsess over what has happened.

I know that. But it is so hard.

Choosing to be happy for my daughter and me

A friend said it best.
"A child can't be happy unless her mother is happy."
Ouch.

I knew this was true. I had spent much of my childhood trying to make my mother happy. Good grades. Blue ribbons. Girl Scouts. (Anything except those damn piano lessons.)

Before she died, my mother used to tell a story about me. When I was in fourth grade, I got hepatitis B. I was out of school for weeks. My concern wasn't the vaccinations that all my classmates had to endure because of my illness. It was whether my mother would have to drop out of classes she was taking for her master's degree.

I knew how badly she wanted that degree. I didn't want to make her unhappier than she already was as a working mother with three school-age children and an alcoholic husband. I just wanted her to be happy.

That memory and the worried looks of my 14-year-old daughter hit me. Dealing with my depression was my responsibility. It wasn't my daughter's job. It wasn't my nurse practitioner's job. It wasn't my therapist's job.

It was my job. I had to do the work. I had to get better if my daughter and I were ever going to have a shot at happiness.

This meant getting my butt out of bed and going to the gym, eating even when I wasn't hungry, taking my medications, answering the phone, shopping, doing laundry, bathing, walking the dog. I had to choose to get better. It wasn't going to just happen.

Then I had an epiphany: Unless there's a gun to my head, everything I do is a choice.

No, I didn't choose to have a brain that doesn't regulate chemicals well. I didn't choose to be depressed.

I did have a choice about how to deal with it, though. This realization seemed remarkable at the time, until I realized all the responsibilities that came with it. I couldn't sit around and play victim anymore. I had to get off the pity pot.

Great.

I had to stop making myself miserable, which meant I had to figure out what was making me miserable and what makes me happy. Most of my misery comes from being busy - "too busy." Oh, I have so much to do. I'm a single working mom. I have to keep the house clean, I have to do laundry, I have to make dinner, I have to go grocery shopping, I have to . . . I have to . . . I have to.

No, I don't.

As long as we have clean underwear, we're OK. We can have soup for dinner. If you don't look down while you're taking a shower, you won't see the ring around the tub. Duh.

When I say "I'm busy," I'm telling people who want my attention - friends who stop to say "hi," who call to tell me who they saw at Starbucks - that whatever I'm doing is way more important than what they have to say. When I stopped saying I was so damn "busy," I stopped being so damned miserable.

Then I had to figure out what makes me really happy. Winning the Lotto. A date with George Clooney. Waking up without wrinkles and gray hair. Another date with George Clooney.

But seriously. What can I do to make myself really happy? Hmmmm. Hmmmm. More hmmmm. A lot more hmmmmm.

Scuba diving. I love scuba diving. No cell phones, no talking, no gravity . . . just pure serenity. My daughter and I sink to the bottom and

I watch her chase nurse sharks and peer into the hulls of sunken wrecks. When we get back on the boat, I pull out my cell phone and text message my friends.

"Saw God on the bottom of the ocean. She says 'hi.'"

I am happy.

Monkeying with meds

I did something stupid. Really stupid.

Before the holidays my medications were adjusted because I was having some "issues." About six weeks ago I saw my nurse practitioner. She said I could stop taking one of the medications but I should continue with another that she had increased over the holidays.

Despite everything I have heard about tinkering with your meds, I went ahead and did it. I lowered the dosage on one medication back down to what it was before the holidays. "Hey, it's just 10 milligrams," I told myself. What could it hurt to go back down to the original dose?

I did not tell anyone that I had done this, especially my therapist and nurse practitioner. I knew I should not have done it. But the holidays were over, and I figured I did not need that extra 10 milligrams.

I was fine for a couple of weeks. Then I got revved up. I lost track of time at work. I jumped out of my chair when someone broke my concentration. I came home from work, and then worked at home. I lost track of time at home. I decided I needed that extra 10 milligrams.

My therapist told me to call my nurse practitioner. I did not make the call because I knew I would have to confess that I had monkeyed with my medications. A month passed. My therapist became annoyingly insistent.

I finally confessed. I figured my nurse practitioner would give me a verbal lickin,' and I could say a bunch of Hail Marys, vow never to do it again and be forgiven. Although my nurse practitioner was much kinder than the nuns in elementary school, she made her point. There can be devastating consequences to messing with your meds. She told me about patients who had done the same thing and she was never able to stabilize them again. These drugs are unlike any others. No one knows how or why they work.

"You don't want to go back to where you were a few years ago, do you?" she asked. No, I definitely do not want to fall back into that black hole ... ever.

I learned my lesson. My illnesses are cunning. Does diabetes convince you that you do not need as much insulin? Will cancer trick you into believing you do not need chemotherapy?

I have illnesses of the brain. These illnesses change the way I think. They want to come out and play. They try to convince me that I am fine and that I don't need medications. You can have a drink or two or eight. You don't need therapy. You don't need all these self-help books. You don't need to listen to people who went to college to learn how to prescribe these drugs.

I know this little voice is real but always wrong. That is all I need to know.

Indulging my mania

If we are only as sick as our secrets, I am still a sick little puppy.

Here is my secret: Sometimes, I like my mania. I like being up - really up. I get a buzz from the energy. I am far more creative, productive and willing to clean the blades of the ceiling fans, the refrigerator, windows, closet, the shed and dust bunnies under my bed.

I like pulling weeds while I talk on the phone. I like renting a chain saw so I can trim trees. I deliberately wait to the last second before leaving for an appointment so I have to rush. I get my money's worth out of my gym membership. My dog, who has learned to run beside my bicycle, is buff.

My therapist has been hounding me about this. I don't want to talk about it. Weeks ago she told me to call my nurse practitioner. I still haven't. I quit drinking, eating wheat and cut back on sugar. Aren't I entitled to some kind of high? Can't I indulge in just a teeny-weeny bit of mania? It feels so good - as long as it doesn't go too high or I do not crash and burn.

Therein lies the problem. I have little control over the crash and burn. Despite the therapy, medications, exercise, good diet and sleep, I know I am increasing my risk of a crash when I indulge my mania. Statistically, the likelihood of another major depression in my lifetime is good.

I took a nap this weekend and I did get into the hammock Sunday afternoon ... for about 10 minutes. On Saturday night I sat still for two hours and watched a movie ... then I was up until 12:30 writing.

A lot of folks would say this is not progress. But for me, just recognizing this is a problem is progress. For many of us with mental illness, changing a behavior is difficult. Especially if it is a compulsive behavior or a behavior fueled by hormones running wild in our brains.

I do have a plan and it does not involve bubble baths, facials or meditation - yet. I am going to re-commit myself to No-Plan Sunday. I plan nothing but church then see what comes my way the rest of the day. I managed to do this for about a year. I do not know why I stopped but it must have been really, really important - like doing my taxes or grocery shopping.

I am going to call my nurse practitioner today. I am going to take a walk at lunch. I am going to remember that life is practice, not perfection.

Pause when agitated

Some things don't come easy for me, like "pause when agitated."

I have heard this phrase for years and it makes a heck of a lot of sense. It works well when my faucet leaks, my bike has a flat or a neighbor's dog makes a deposit on my front lawn.

It is not easy for someone who is bipolar, like me, to pause when agitated. When agitation turns to anger, pausing - even for a moment - is a monumental feat. I have been working on techniques to handle my anger for years.

I have been told to bite my lips to keep my mouth closed. To not be sarcastic and to cut off contact with those who are sarcastic. To end a heated conversation with "I think we should agree to disagree."

If that does not work, I should physically remove myself from the target of my anger and have no contact until I have defused and have calmly studied my role. Great advice but unnatural acts if you are mentally ill.

Of all my emotions, anger is the most toxic. Some say that for many women, depression is anger turned inward. For me, getting rid of anger is a process that begins by "purging" myself - physically. I exercise as hard and as fast as I can. I get in the car, roll up the windows, holler everything I would have loved to have said, and then turn up Led Zeppelin as loud as my speakers allow.

When my heart rate returns to normal I write and talk about it. I try to meditate, stretch and pray. Then I make a pot roast and fix myself a mug of hot chocolate before bed. It can take days for the emotional hangover to lift. I do not sleep well. I have nightmares. My thoughts race. Then I get on my knees every night and - through clenched teeth - ask God to give that person everything I desire for myself. I do that until my TMJ kicks in or my anger dissolves.

This is the crossroads where daily life intersects mental illness. Healthy brains move on down the road. My brain sits at the intersection, stuck in neutral, revving the engine. If I work hard enough and stay on my side of the street, the rage dissolves into resentment, a lesson learned and, finally, an apology.

I must always remember that people who do not know I am mentally ill and even those who do are not responsible for my behavior. I am.

Side effects and tight jeans

Imagine you have an illness and the medicine you need will drive a stake through your self-esteem.

For women this means gaining weight. For men it means, "reduced sexual desire, erectile dysfunction, and difficulty achieving orgasm or ejaculation," according to the Mayo Clinic Web site.

Many medications cause side effects. We know when we see a bald woman that she is probably undergoing chemotherapy. Although the side effects of chemotherapy are awful, they can cure the underlying cancer. We do not pass judgment on her illness or medications.

With mental illness, we know we likely will be judged and so we hide our disease. The side effects of our medications, though, can't be hidden. And those side effects can, and often do, make the underlying illness worse.

A bipolar woman who has gained 15 pounds is not going to tell you that her antipsychotic medication caused the weight gain. A man with performance issues is not going to divulge to his partner that his antidepressant causes some embarrassing side effects.

Which brings me to my medications, my scale and my stretched-out skinny jeans.

Several months ago when I was having some manic episodes my nurse practitioner put me back on an antipsychotic medication that helps me right my sails and sleep soundly. It also causes weight gain. It was only 3 pounds, but that was on top of the 5 pounds I gained last year on another medication. That's 8 pounds. No big deal, right? Wrong. It is a huge deal to me. Go ahead, call me vain, self-absorbed and shallow. These medication-induced love handles make me very unhappy.

I called my nurse practitioner and told her I wanted to stop taking the drug - now. She agreed as long as I promised to call if I started feeling out of whack again. The pounds are slowly melting away. The jeans are still a little snug but I am not sighing as much when I look in the mirror. I feel plumb - not plump - again, and happy.

Depression in a bottle

Now that the most wonderful time of the year is finally over, it's time to reluctantly ponder our receipts, waistlines and resolutions.

If you are mentally ill like me but find after-Christmas sales and hot chocolate irresistible, you probably should not do this much pondering in one sitting. I know what I should do: Freeze the credit cards in a block of ice, avoid eye contact with steaming mugs of hot chocolate and stop grazing.

As for resolutions, I have one suggestion: Quit drinking alcohol. I know it sounds drastic and difficult. Besides my medications, nothing has helped me better manage my depression and bipolar more than sobriety.

For starters, sobriety will help your financial and waistline woes. Booze is not cheap, especially if you're buying. It is not low-calorie - even the hard stuff. Why drink wine without crackers, cheese, bread, pasta, a thick steak or chocolate chip cookies? Doesn't beer taste better with a hamburger, fries, chicken wings, chili or chocolate chip cookies? You can't have one without the other.

Then there is the biology of booze in a mentally ill brain. I wish I could tell you in English exactly what happens. I know this: Researchers have found that alcohol lowers - depresses - serotonin and norepinephrine levels. These are brain chemicals that regulate emotions and feelings. That means alcohol is actually a depressant, no matter how much fun dancing on the bar seemed last night.

People with depression, like me, typically have too little or too much of certain brain chemicals, including serotonin and norepinephrine. Since my brain already has problems producing these chemicals, why would I want to drink something that makes it more difficult for my brain to produce these chemicals in healthy amounts?

Because washing down a plate of hot chocolate chip cookies with a few Kahlua and Creams makes me happy! Until my serotonin and norepinephrine tank - then I become more depressed than ever. Alcohol also relaxes my inhibitions, which means a thought - such as suicide - is more likely to become an action when I drink.

"But I am not an alcoholic. I drink socially," many of us say. Experts at the Substance Abuse and Mental Health Services Administration say it does not take as much drinking for us to become abusers as it does for people without mental illness.

"It is unclear if anyone with a severe mental illness, such as schizophrenia or bipolar disorder, can drink socially over time without running into difficulties, but most who drink (probably over 90 percent) either develop problems related to alcohol or opt for abstinence."

That is good enough for me. Besides, chocolate chip cookies taste much better with milk.

Weathering winter

I had a nightmare last week. I was told I was being transferred from Florida to Michigan ... in December.

My first thought was not of telling my daughter she would have to leave her school and friends, or of trying to sell my house, or even what my job would be in Michigan.

It was seasonal affective disorder. I remember pleading: "Don't you know what this means? This will kill me. I have seasonal affective disorder. Please don't do this." Then I was in Michigan, looking out a window at a pile of deflated, aging snow in what passes for daylight for five long months in Michigan.

I woke up. "It was just a dream ... just a dream ... not going to happen ... just a dream."

If you do not have seasonal affective disorder this probably sounds silly. If you have seasonal affective disorder this dream probably makes you nervous, sad, anxious, or even more depressed. The reality is I live in West Palm Beach, Fla. It is December. The temperature is 79 degrees today and the sky is blue.

Moving here 24 years ago changed my life. Winter was hell for me up north, especially January, February and March. Nine hours of flat, cold daylight, 15 hours of darkness.

Still I get that funky feeling during the Florida winter. I chalk it up to holiday excess, hormones and snowbirds clogging the roads. This year it seems worse. It started after Halloween, when the days became shorter. I thought it was impossible to get seasonal affective disorder in the tropics. It never crossed my mind. Although rare, it can happen.

Researchers believe there are three causes: A disruption in your circadian rhythm, the physiological process that regulates your internal clock and tells you when to sleep and wake; an increase in production of a sleep-related hormone called melatonin; a decrease in the production of serotonin, a natural brain chemical that affects mood.

Light plays a role - as does the lack of light. Shaving several hours of daylight off a day, even in the tropics, can trigger SAD symptoms. Although rare, it can happen.

I am not going to diagnose myself with SAD. For all I know it could be the holidays, hormones or the snowbirds clogging traffic. But I am keeping an eye on this funk and will take my subconscious to the beach.

Facing fear

I think God is trying to tell me something.

This morning I got into the car to go to the gym and the song that started along with the car was David Bowie's *Pressure*. It didn't start in the middle of the song. It was cued to the beginning so I could hear the whole thing. Then, I walked into the gym and Lenny Kravitz was wailing *"I want to get away, I want to fly away. ..."*

Coincidence? I think not. I have been struggling the past couple of months, trying to stay on an even keel. I keep heeling over, stretched out over the gunwale, pulling hard on the tiller. My boss asked how I was, and I told her. "Tired. I can't keep running at this pace."

"It's self-inflicted, you know. You don't have to run at this pace. You can slow down," she said. She was right. She was not pushing me. No one was pushing me. Why am I doing this to myself?

Because I am scared. Four things scare me - sharks, cancer, being extracted from a car wreck by the jaws of life and being unemployed. It's the last one that's got me. A television, permanently tuned to CNN, hangs from the newsroom ceiling, just waiting to tell me about more layoffs. Those poor folks in Chicago, Dow Chemical, Sprint, Sun Microsystems and Merrill Lynch. Last week, The Tribune Co., owner of the *Chicago Tribune*, filed for bankruptcy.

I know I have nothing to fear but fear itself. But fear itself is scaring the heck out of me and making me sick. I avoid my fear by working - in the office, house, gym and yard. Friday night I worked until 8:30 p.m. Saturday morning I got up and rented a chain saw from Home Depot.

When I feel that I have no control over what is going on around me, I get busy. I cannot just sit still and be afraid.

My therapist tells me that if I sit still and indulge the fear, look at it rationally, I will be able to dissect it. I will discover that some of it is not real and what is real, I can handle - as long as I do not push myself into a depression with all my fear and busyness.

Intellectually, that sounds great. But I can't stop the busyness or the tape that accompanies it: "See, if you had worked harder all these years you wouldn't have to worry about being laid off. If you had sprayed those hedges you wouldn't be slinging a chain saw on your day off. If you had saved more money, if you had ... if you had ... if you had. ..."

Now I am afraid and belittled. Not healthy.

I am waiting for a call from my nurse practitioner. We are going to talk about adjusting my meds. In the meantime, God has pulled another little joke on me: The endless loop of *Feliz Navidad* that has been playing in my head has been replaced with Bono singing *Beautiful Day*.

Money: The great divide

The top 1 percent of the U.S. population owns about one-third of the country's net worth.

I am definitely not in that minority. That has become obvious in the last couple of weeks with every bill that arrives, accompanied by waves of emotions, none of which are pleasant. When the initial sting wears off and I have withdrawn my petition for martyrdom I am left with an overwhelming urge to blame someone, anyone. Sometimes it is me, but it is much more fun to find someone else.

Right now I'm giving the evil eye to the Richard Fulds of Wall Street. Fuld is the former CEO of the former Lehman Brothers who somehow thought he deserved $73 million for leading the company as it went under.

What could these guys have done while driving their companies into the ground that made them believe they deserved this kind of money? I bet none of them has ever missed a car payment or scrounged around in his couch for change. They are not clipping coupons or wondering how to get creative with the leftover chicken. They probably think Goodwill is a blessing given to men at Christmas.

Shall I go on?

Sure, this soundtrack makes me feel better, but it is time to turn it off. Obsessing on what separates me from the 1 percent is the stuff that my depression is made of: anger, rage, resentment, regret, remorse, intense anxiety and stress.

I am so accustomed to doing this that it is now a reflex. There's that lady with the Prada purse, and the wife with the husband who believes diamonds really are a girl's best friend, and the women in tennis outfits at the grocery store on a weekday afternoon.

It's easy - actually fun - to do, especially when rich politicians refer to us as the folks living on "Main Street," like we are some kind of homogenized, penny-pinching, mac-and-cheese eaters.

This must stop. This kind of thinking is toxic. It makes the income divide wider and my mood uglier. Anger, resentment and manufacturing disparity are luxuries I cannot afford.

Instead I am going to focus on what I have in common with people, even if it is a simple as "Hey, I have a Prada knock-off! Aren't they great-looking bags?"

It's a start.

It's just stuff

I drove my mother to hospice. Halfway down the driveway we stopped and I asked her whether she wanted to go back in one last time. She did not look at me. She looked at the house where she had raised three children and lived for nearly 40 years and said, "No, it's just a roof with a bunch of stuff under it."

This was our home that she had filled with antiques she refinished, chairs she caned, her needlepoint pillows, the black and white childhood silhouette portraits of us three kids, the Christmas ornaments, her recipe collection and boxes and boxes of family photos.

Suddenly, it was all just "stuff." I have been thinking about this lately as the nation frets about how we are going to pay for all of the stuff under our roofs, and the houses themselves.

Money, relationships and illness are my emotional deal-breakers. I have staggered through relationship and illness catastrophes. I did neither well and ended up in an emotional wasteland.

Faced with my parents' fatal illnesses, I stoked my mania - redefining "frenetic" - to avoid the pain of their imminent deaths. As for relationships, all I can say is with all my experience you would think I would have some skill at handling the aftermath. Instead, I stop eating and sink into depression.

Now, it's financial insecurity. Money, and the lack of, is probably our nation's biggest mental health threat. I have not looked at the balances of my 401(k) or other retirement investments in two weeks. The last time I checked a ball of anxiety contracted in my chest.

I will not ignore reality, as much as I would like to. But I cannot torture myself with what-ifs and maybes. I do not want to go through this economic depression in a depression. When a wave of fear sweeps over me, that is not the time to turn on C-Span and listen to testimony about financial Armageddon. I wait until I can calm my fears, and then I go through the pile of bills.

I don't bury my head in the sand. I have to be honest with myself and my credit card. I made some stupid, extravagant purchases, like those gorgeous red patent-leather pointy-toed shoes with the 4-inch heels. Just because the money and the line of credit was there does not mean I had to spend it.

Somehow, a lot of us came to believe that we needed to spend it. Fancy cars, McMansions, $200 haircuts, granite countertops and gorgeous red patent-leather pointy-toed shoes with 4-inch heels. Now we are paying for the roof-with-a-bunch-of-stuff-under-it with sleepless nights, shortness of breath, headaches, worry, tears and, God forbid, depression.

I suspect the economy will get worse before it gets better. I need to feel better before it gets worse. Regret and guilt do me no good right now and "now" needs to be my focus. I don't know why, but stewing on the dumb stuff I bought and did during the fat years feels good in a bad way. I tell myself that this is my old, sick thinking. It feels comfortable because it is familiar. That does not mean it is healthy.

Depression is cunning and insidious, almost as if it has a life of its own and controls your thoughts in order to make itself strong. Avoiding thoughts that fuel depression and mania is tough while your 401(k) tanks. So I am going to make the best of this. My credit card and I will not repeat history. Somewhere among all the minus signs and down turned arrows is the lesson that my mother tried to teach me.

It's just stuff.

Listening and being

About the most annoying thing you can say to a person in clinical depression is a sentence that begins with "You should."

Trust me, we know we should be doing a lot of things. If we could we would. But being told what we should do only will make us withdraw even more.

I dislike "you should" sentences even when I am happy. I just don't like being told what to do. Brings out the Irish in me. When I was in my last depression I learned that nothing says "you don't get it" more than a "you should" statement.

You should: Get up and walk the dog; eat; stop eating; sleep; stop sleeping so much; take a shower; clean the house; go to a movie; go shopping; go to the gym ...

I know this sounds harsh to those who really care, love us and live with us. We know you are trying to help. I know that when I am in a depression I should not be alone - even though I act like I want to be alone and I am not even remotely fun or interesting to be around. And you are there for me.

Knowing this, I offer two how-to suggestions. The first is how to be around a person with depression who is able and wants to talk. This may sound like a no-brainer but it is not. Just listen. Although I am a reporter and get paid to listen and write what I hear, I did not learn how to listen until my mother was dying five years ago.

After reading every possible Google search on colon cancer, I found an article on the art of listening to the very sick. Listening does not mean giving unsolicited advice. I don't have to answer every "why?" asked by someone who is very sick. Sometimes they just want someone to hear their pain - not judge it.

Listening does not mean I have to solve every problem or take responsibility for what needs to be done. With every problem solved or responsibility met we get a sense of accomplishment. Take that away from the sick and they feel worthless and a burden.

Listening to someone who is depressed is awkward. It goes against what we have been taught about helping others. Helping means doing something. Listening feels like you are doing nothing.

So, what should you say around someone who is depressed and does not want to talk? If you have been in a similar situation, share your experience, strength and hope. We need empathy, not sympathy or pity. Say something encouraging. Blame the depression, not us. Turn every pregnant pause and awkward silence into an opportunity to speak with your eyes. Let someone with depression know that you are not uncomfortable with them. And never, ever start a sentence with "you should."

Worrying about the weather

The Weather Channel scares the hell out of me. If you have lived through a hurricane you know what I'm talking about. If it is August or September and I walk into a room and The Weather Channel is on, I stop talking, walking, thinking and turn my full attention to the screen.

I quickly inhale, hold it and feel the knot in my chest. The meteorologist could be talking about golf in Palm Springs but I know there must be a hurricane out there.

Why else would you watch The Weather Channel in Florida during August or September? The weather is always the same: Hot. Humid. Highs in the mid-90s. Chance of afternoon thunderstorms. So there must be a hurricane out there if The Weather Channel is on.

Then I start worrying. I need more Tapcons. I should really buy a chain saw. Get that tree trimmed. Buy food. Make ice. Wash all the clothes. I start to worry.

The only thing I don't worry about is batteries. I hoard batteries when I turn on my hurricane worry switch. I have more batteries in my freezer than ice cream and pizzas.

Worrying is bad - really, really bad - for my depression and hypomania. It has taken me years to learn this. It goes against everything in my being. In the Midwestern, Irish Catholic household I grew up in, worrying was a virtue. It showed how truly much you care. If you were a really caring person, like my mother, worrying was an instinct.

For me, worrying is like eating potato chips. I cannot have just one. After I finish worrying about my house being blown away I worry about my finances.

Then I start worrying about my daughter's looming college bills, my retirement and the economy. Next thing I know I am worrying about paying for her wedding. She just turned 16. Oh, how could I forget? I worry about her driving.

While this worrying is going on I can practically feel the worry spigot open in my brain, flooding it with nasty hormones, proteins and other bad chemicals that bring on anxiety.

Last week after five days of obsessing over hurricane advisories when I should have been enjoying the Olympics, I woke up one morning with the worst episode of anxiety I have experienced since my last major depression 2 1/2 years ago. I questioned and doubted everything and everyone in my life, including myself.

I reminded myself that this is how it starts. I have learned a lot about controlling my thoughts in the past couple of years. It's called cognitive behavioral therapy. So, I decided to try some of these tools. I called a friend, who straightened me out about how unrealistic these thoughts were. I decided to cut down on the caffeine. I visualized a really slick fly rod with one of those beautiful reels and I slowly and calmly reeled myself in.

27

Then I remembered the out-of-the-mouths-of-babes comment my daughter made years ago when I was worried about something.

"You know, worrying shows God you don't trust him."

Drinking to beat the blues?

Here is a paradox we are seeing a lot of these days.

Money is the No. 1 cause of stress for Americans. Stress substantially increases the risk of depression. Alcohol is a depressant. Alcohol is expensive.

So, why would you spend your money on alcohol if you have depression and money problems?

You are making your depression and your money problems worse.

The logically illogical reason: We love to cry in our beer - even if the beer is the reason we are crying. As the economy tanks, we get tanked.

The numbers prove it. Budweiser brewer Anheuser-Busch saw second-quarter profits increase nearly 2 percent to $689 million.

About the worst thing you can do when the bank forecloses on your home, you lose your job and you've maxed out your credit cards is hit the bottle.

Here is why: Alcohol increases stress hormones.

"Why people should engage in an activity that produces effects similar to those they are trying to relieve is a paradox that we do not yet understand," said Dr. Enoch Gordis, former director of the National Institute on Alcohol Abuse and Alcoholism.

If the science of alcohol, stress and depression is not enough to make you quit, consider your pocketbook.

Americans drink enough every year for each one of us to down seven bottles of liquor, 12 bottles of wine and 230 cans of beer.

That means even the most frugal drinker will spend about $500 every year on alcohol.

But that number quickly doubles, triples or goes even higher if you drink more, drink more expensive alcohol, drink at a bar or pick up the tab for the next round.

Now that's depressing.

I am not saying that everyone who loses a job, a house or good credit score should quit drinking, but I gave it up. It isn't always easy. After a stressful day at work, a glass of wine - or two or three - sounds really good. I have trained myself to think it through - all the way through.

Yes, initially I will feel better, more relaxed. Then, alcohol triggers the release of more stress hormones.

There is also the stress from saying things I regret later, the hangover, my empty wallet and, of course, the warning to "avoid alcohol completely" on my prescriptions.

I look at it like this: We all have a lifetime quota of booze we can safely drink. Most don't hit it. Others are way over.

Those of us with depression have smaller quotas, and I already have hit mine. Alcohol is a luxury I cannot afford.

The little blue pill box

On Sunday nights, when I am trying to figure what I can wear to work that does not need ironing, I fill my little blue pill box for the week. Three pills in each little box. Twenty-one pills a week.

"Man," I think. "That's a lot of pills. I really, really, really wish I didn't have to take these things."

Then I remember Bruce Stutz and his "brain zaps."

Stutz is a writer who decided to wean himself off Effexor with no medical assistance. He wrote about the experience in a *New York Times Sunday Magazine* story on May 6, 2007.

"I was in a pharmacological Catch-22," Stutz wrote. "The only way to know whether my depression would return if I went off my antidepressants was to go off my antidepressant and risk depression."

His reasons for doing it himself: It had been four years since he had seen his psychiatrist, who let Stutz walk out the door without any discussion about his antidepressant. Stutz "did not want to return to the place, physically and mentally, where I had gone through so much pain." And he could not afford more sessions.

Among his withdrawal symptoms: Sleeplessness, dizziness, nausea, disorientation, restlessness, heavy sweats, chills, tingling in his shoulders and hands, leg spasms, irritability and awakening himself with screams so loud, "that it seemed to echo in the room long after I sat up awake."

But what scared me most were Stutz's blinding "brain zaps."

"I felt a quick spasm in my head as if an electrical current had suddenly been sent through a circuit somewhere inside my brain. Two more followed in quick succession. With each came a wave of nausea."

Why would anyone in his right mind put himself through this? I like my brain. Sure, there was a time in my life when - with the help of the Grateful Dead - I killed a lot of brain cells.

Today, I make dang sure that I take no risks with my brain. My nurse practitioner does not let me leave her office without making our next appointment. If I could not afford to see her and wanted to get off my antidepressants, I still would call and ask for her help.

If I could not afford my medications, I would call the local health department or check out the program Montel Williams pushes, the Partnership for Prescription Assistance, which provides free medications to those who can't afford them. Heck, I would even call the drug company and ask for help. I would no more stop taking my medications than I would stop brushing my teeth.

It took two months for Stutz to get off Effexor. His depression did not return and he has had no reason to go back on antidepressants. I, too, want to get off these drugs. That is my goal, someday. But part of my recovery from depression is admitting that I need help. There are some things I cannot - and should not - do alone.

The promises of Proverbs

There was a time when I secretly scoffed at the people in line at the bookstore waiting to pay for self-help books.

Puh-leez. Your life is so pathetic and you are so clueless that you need some sanctimonious, money-grubbing guru to tell you how to solve your problems? You poor soul.

I lost that attitude pretty quick. When you're in enough pain - physical or mental - you will try just about anything to feel better. Even self-help books.

There are some wonderful books about depression. You can read them in the privacy of your home without judgment from self-righteous, pompous fools like me standing behind you at the bookstore.

When you have a stigmatized illness such as depression or bipolar disorder there is much comfort in meeting others - even on the page of a book - who have endured the same desperation and have come out the other side. For me, learning about the physiology of depression and the chemistry of the brain gave me tremendous relief. These writings convinced me I was not weak or lazy. I was sick.

Then I found the other books. These were not written for or about the mentally ill, but they gave me insight, hope and a new way of thinking about and living with depression.

From the teachings of the Dalai Lama - a guy I knew only from the movie *Caddyshack* - I learned change was inevitable and what I was going through would not last. From William Styron I learned great literature could be born of mental illness. I dabbled in Melody Beattie and Eckhart Tolle.

But I have gained my greatest strength from reading The Book of Proverbs. I was never much into the Bible. Of course I never sat down and read it. It just made me uncomfortable. I preferred sleep, bacon and eggs on Sunday mornings.

I figured I had read most of John Grisham's books, I might as well give the Bible a chance. Mental illness has a way of prying open a closed mind.

Wisdom, knowledge, humility, honesty, simplicity, respect and compassion. To stay healthy needed a new way to think and act. I found it.

Like Baskin-Robbins, The Book of Proverbs has 31 ways to make your life better.

Now, in the mornings, after I take my medications and skim the headlines, I read a proverb.

Some days I forget. Still, it has become enough of a routine to have left my Bible looking well-used. That is one of the blessings of my depression.

The inner voice of my mania

For a reason unknown to me, I decided to organize my 31st high school class reunion. (We skipped our 30th.)

In the midst of it all, I learned I might not have a job by year's end. Buyouts. Layoffs.

My thoughts are racing again. When you are bipolar, racing thoughts are a part of life. It's like the guy on those car commercials who whizzes through the fine print of the car lease faster than you can listen. All day, all night that guy blathers on in my head at warp speed. The thoughts consume me. They are utterly inane one moment, then monumental the next. They will overwhelm me if I am not careful.

I take medications for my racing thoughts and they work well. Still, when I let life creep up on me, the race begins again.

It sounds like this: Name tags...on the list...medical benefits...how will I afford my meds?...cut the grass... What about centerpieces? Just go to Home Depot and buy a bunch of plants...get ribbon...blue and yellow...school colors...bring a Sharpie, tape and push pins...probably need them...the map...shoes...definitely need new shoes with that dress... gold or silver?...COBRA, how long with that cover us?...what if Kealy gets sick?...or has an accident...can't touch the 401(k)...maybe Howie would cut the grass while I'm out of town...on the list...DJ...gotta find a DJ...call Martha about a DJ...on the list...do the math...100 people at $40 a head = $4,000...food $23 a head...tent rental is...what about unemployment?... can I get unemployment?...maybe refinance the house...what's the going rate?...on the list...10 months the car is paid off...how much is a DJ?...no disco...all that paperwork on your desk... write three columns and two stories before Thursday

...Maybe I could teach...paralegal...private investigator...have to quit therapy...weird dreams lately...gold or silver?...what is the PIN number for that credit card...is that chicken thawed out yet?...grill it?...probably rain...did I turn off the coffee pot?...feed the dog...there's no gas in the car...who's having a shoe sale?...coupons...haven't been unemployed since I was 14...worrying shows God you don't trust him...the newsroom will be so quiet...schedule a mammogram NOW...call Marsha...send John the check...e-mail to Holly...no way I can afford my meds without insurance...the front tire on the bike is leaking...new tube...on the list... need a weed whacker...miss the yard guy...can't afford it...how much is a weed whacker...pawnshop?...where is a pawn shop?...what if it's a stolen weed whacker?...on the list...five pounds...just five pounds before the reunion...gold or silver?

...this job thing is completely out of my hands...don't worry about things you can't control ...pray...pray...pray...God hasn't dragged you this far to drop you now...opportunity...maybe it's an opportunity...doesn't feel like an opportunity...what time does the mall open? Macy's coupon... don't spend money on shoes now...when does the dog need shots? Cheap shots at the shelter...when do we need our teeth cleaned? Pray harder... flood insurance payment is late...did I get a rebate check from the IRS?

...Losing a job is not the end of the world...lot of people are worse off...you can do this...it's all going to be OK...you'll get her through college somehow...forget about awnings for the front windows...you're not a loser...it's just business...will miss so many people... take the dress with you when you shop for shoes...nail polish...what if it rains?...scared...I'm scared...wish mom was still alive...it's all gonna be OK...it's all gonna be OK...it's all gonna be OK...gold or silver?

Wanting to live...finally

I had a big scare last week. I was lying on the couch, watching yet another episode of *Law & Order* with my dog asleep beside me. I fell asleep. Not unusual.

A short while later I realized the program was over but I was so comfortable and so tired ... why not just sleep tonight on the couch?

No, you've got to get up and wash off this makeup, brush your teeth and take your meds.

No, live it up. Sleep on the couch tonight.

No, you will wake up with raccoon eyes, really bad breath and behind on your meds.

I got up, walked to the kitchen and it hit me. A very strong smell of gas. I looked at the stove. The knob showed it was on but there was no flame. I turned it off, opened the windows, awakened Dog and ran outside.

Oh my God. I could have died. Thank God my daughter was sleeping at a friend's and I have a thing about sleeping in my makeup and my meds are in the kitchen.

I almost died! I was numb. I almost died. I almost died. Thank you, God, thank you, God, thank you, God.

Then it hit me. There was a time in my life when dying sounded like a very good solution. A time when I spent a good deal of time thinking about whether my hybrid produced enough carbon monoxide to kill me.

But now, I REALLY want to live. Really, really, really want to live. I want to live to be 100. I want to learn to surf. I want to be the grandmother who lets her grandkids eat a bowl of M&Ms with milk for breakfast.

I definitely don't want to die.

If suicide has ever been a real option, you can appreciate the juxtaposition of wanting to live and wanting to die. When you want to kill yourself, you obsess about pills, vodka, guns, hoses and tall buildings. These are very private thoughts. When I was in a depression and told my therapist but for my daughter I wouldn't be here, she made me sign a contract.

It seemed absurd. By signing I was promising to call a suicide hotline if my thoughts were turning to action.

"You have got to be kidding me," I told her. "You really think a piece of paper is going to mean a damn thing to me if I want to kill myself? I mean, come on, how are you going to enforce it?"

But I did think about it. And I thought about Sister Matthew and what the nuns at St. Stephen's told us kids about suicide and burning in hell for eternity. I thought through the entire thing. I realized the pain I would cause those who cared about me would be greater than the pain I was in.

My desperation was so great I could not bear the thought of forcing it on anyone. I thought about that stupid contract. And I just couldn't do it.

And now, I definitely don't want to. And that feels good, even if it took a big scare to wake me up.

NOW: *The final frontier*

My new mantra is "now."

The company I work for is downsizing. I do not know if I will have a job in two months.

The monkeys in my manic mind are frantic. They won't stop. Some are two years ahead incessantly turning back flips in place. The rest are stuck in the past, screeching at what should have been.

This is not good. This will make me sick.

Two years ago, before I learned to use the tools to build a healthy mind, I would have served those monkeys a double-espresso and cheered them on. But after coming out of a major depression, I learned I am the master of those monkeys.

With the tools I have today, my first reaction to the news was this: I need to take care of myself. I need to stay healthy. I need to be gentle with myself. I need to think of Chevy Chase in *Caddyshack* chanting "na-na-na-na-na-na-na" but change that meditation to "now-now-now-now-now."

When my mind fast-forwards to the future and begins worrying about how I will pay for my medications, I pull myself back and tell myself, "Now, right now, at this very moment in time, you have plenty of your medications and you have insurance to pay for more."

Today, I tell myself, your daughter is two years away from college. Today, your mortgage is paid. Today, your 401(k) is intact. At this very moment, the AC works and the checks aren't bouncing.

Now. Stay present. Focus on this very moment in time. When your brain races ahead, reel it back in. Concentrate on what you hear right now, what you see right now, what you smell right now.

Right now, at this moment in time, you are safe, healthy and employed. Sprinting back and forth between the future and the past will make you very anxious. When I am stressed and anxious the chemicals in my brain get out of whack. This is bad for anyone, but toxic for someone with depression or a bipolar illness.

Yesterday morning, I took my dog to the beach - a place that always makes me present. But I found my mind wandering. I didn't hear the waves, smell the salt air, feel my toes sinking into the sand or see the shells.

Then I saw my dog - "Dog" - sprinting towards me. I could have sworn he had a smile on his face. I snapped out of it and realized that he lives his entire life in the present. He eats only when he is hungry, sleeps when he is tired, drinks from the toilet when he is thirsty, scratches when he has an itch, shoves his cold nose under my arm when he needs affection.

Dog has figured it out.

The anxiety of awakening

I woke this morning before my alarm. I heard a steady flow of raindrops pop off the awning outside my bedroom. This is a sound I love - especially in the midst of a long drought that nearly killed my budding backyard tropical jungle.

Normally I would open the curtains, climb back into bed with my dog and give myself permission to watch the rain and get to the office a few minutes late. Normally, I would think how blessed I am to have a nice little house, a comfortable bed, a beautiful 16-year-old daughter whose nose isn't pierced, a faithful pup, a job I still love and - best of all - it was Friday.

That would be how I would normally feel if my brain was working the way it is supposed to. But not this morning.

Instead, I opened my eyes to overwhelming, untraceable anxiety. Like a drunk with a hangover, I did an inventory of last night. Did I do or say anything that would make me feel this way? No. Is the mortgage paid? Yes. Did I have a fight with my daughter? No. Did I remember to take out the garbage and return the overdue movie? Yes.

I try to remember my dreams. The bad dreams are back. They are not nightmares but they are bad. So bad that while I am having one of them I remember thinking, "Wow, this is a bad dream" then falling right back into it.

"You haven't done anything wrong," I tell myself after my inventory.

I realize that everything around me - all the physical objects - is the same as it was last month when I felt grateful and serene. Nothing has changed. Except the chemicals in my brain.

I woke up like this for many, many years. I got used to it, actually comfortable with it. It's a long-term, low-grade depression called dysthemia. I thought that was just the way life is.

Today, two years after a major depression, a diagnosis and a regimen of therapy and medications - I stopped waking up in an emotional purgatory. I wake up cheerful, like those happy-go-lucky, well-rested actors stretching in those sleep aid commercials.

Until today.

But instead of surrendering and accepting this anxiety I decided to fight it. I pull out all the tools I have learned from my therapist, friends and those mostly unread self-help books stacked in my bedroom. I eat, take my meds, have a cup of decaf, say a little prayer and tell myself over and over that feelings aren't facts.

I give myself permission to get to the office a few minutes late and I walk my dog to the dog park. Then, I decide to start the day over.

Judging mental illness in court

A few years ago, I testified in a trial. I was not suing or being sued. I was simply a witness.

Opposing counsel tried to discredit my testimony by dragging my mental illnesses into court. The attorney who had subpoenaed me assured me that the judge would not allow it. It wasn't relevant, he said.

The judge allowed it.

After a few questions, the judge changed his mind and told the jury to disregard what they had heard.

I was angry and embarrassed. My decision to seek help confirmed that I had a problem. Maybe if I had not sought help, that lawyer would not have been able to ask those questions. Seeking help had nailed me.

I have seen this in court before. A lot. I covered the court beat for about 12 years. Sometimes I saw it in divorce cases. Often I saw it in criminal cases.

The most memorable example was the William Kennedy Smith rape case. Late on a Friday afternoon - a time when it is nearly impossible to reach anyone for comment - Smith's attorneys filed a motion for the accuser's medical records.

Among the reasons: The records would show that the woman was "suffering from a psychiatric disorder," that could explain why she "made a false accusation against Mr. Smith." They also wanted to know whether the woman had ever been in drug or alcohol rehab.

Don't you know that mentally ill people are liars, and alcoholics and addicts cannot be trusted? We are lousy parents, lazy spouses and unpredictable employees. God forbid you ever seek help and some kind of medical record - "subpoena bait" - is created.

This is why many people with medical insurance pay out of pocket for psychiatrists, prescriptions and therapy. They don't want to create a record of their mental illness.

I absolutely agree that some of us are reckless - even dangerous. Some of us are lazy and unpredictable. These can be good reasons to change custody or dismiss charges. But many of us are not. We are simply sick. Seeking help is smart. It shows good judgment. When we get help, we get better. And when we are better we can become fine parents, workers and citizens.

There is a line that should not be crossed in court. Every judge and lawyer draws his or her own line. Yes, there is case law to guide these decisions. But too often, the will to win, belittle or get even consumes what is just and fair. Despite a judge's best efforts, what a jury or the public hears cannot be unheard.

Even though the judge in the William Kennedy Smith case did not allow the woman's medical records into evidence, the lawyers' implication that she may have been treated for a "psychiatric disorder" suggested that she was cuckoo - and not to be believed.

Smith's attorney, Roy Black, hammered home that point while cross-examining the woman.

"You went to see your psychologist that morning?" Black asked about the morning after the incident.

"Yes."

"One of your routine appointments?" Black asked sarcastically.

"Yes."

This kind of behavior in court forces mental illness underground. It fuels the stigma and prevents people from seeking help.

It is not justice.

A taste of gratitude

There is an upside to depression.

When you finally come out of it - and you will - you are left with a kind of gratitude you did not know you were capable of. The most ordinary sound, image or touch can be strikingly pleasing.

At this time two years ago I was at the bottom of a deep dark hole. I had no interest in food. I drove in silence, no radio or CDs. I tried shopping for shoes and watching *There's Something About Mary*. Nothing. My brain had flat-lined.

I could see no light at the end of the tunnel. I couldn't even see the tunnel. Days melted together. A nap was all I wanted. Then, one evening as I drove to a friend's home, I felt it lifting. I will never forget the gratitude I felt at that moment.

I covered my mouth and cried. It had been a month since I began taking antidepressants. Maybe they were finally working.

The sun was setting. The clouds were pink. The temperature was perfect. The waterfront was stunning. I was well. Just like that.

Twenty minutes later it was gone. In a flash I was back at the bottom of my black hole - again. I was stunned. That was cruel, I thought. Very, very cruel.

These are the moments you think about giving up. This is too hard. I cannot do this. It's not worth it. These medications don't work. I am too tired. What's the point?

The point is, you will get better. No matter how desperate I felt, I believed the people who had been there and promised me I would get better.

Slowly, very slowly, over the next month, I scaled the walls of my black hole and peeked over the edge. I was terrified that I would fall again. I didn't. I slowly climbed out, got to my feet and began living again. This time it was really over

It was then I began to feel grateful.

There is some kind of symbiotic relationship between gratitude and happiness. I cannot be happy unless I am grateful. I cannot be grateful until I am happy. Gratitude is the gift of depression. I would have preferred to find it another way, but I am grateful I found it anyway.

I had never wanted to go to work so badly. Music, food and the feel of my dog snuggled against my chest - never had I felt so grateful for these things. Driving my daughter to the mall, cooking, cleaning and folding clothes. Working in the yard. Going to the gym. Everything was a pleasure.

And still is.

The price - and cost - of medication

I took economics in college. It was not my favorite class. I have the transcript to prove it. I vaguely remember something about

microeconomics and pricing and a marketing mix and blah, blah, blah
…

Obviously, the marketing folks at the pharmaceutical companies thoroughly understand this stuff. And they are making a fortune at pricing mental health medications.

I just don't get it. I don't understand how I can get a three-month supply of any antidepressant through my company's mail-in prescription plan for $40.

Meanwhile uninsured folks who must pay the market price are paying four, five, sometimes six times as much as I do for the very same medication.

I know it has something to do with the cost of manufacturing, distributing and marketing the drugs. Still, that doesn't explain why a month's supply of 20 milligrams Adderall costs $138.24 at Wal-Mart and $159.99 at Walgreen's just a few miles away.

How come a month's supply of 150 milligrams tablets of Trazodone cost $14.99 at CVS and $67.50 at another pharmacy up the road? We have a similar situation with a month's supply of 150 milligrams tablet Wellbutrin XL, which costs $128.97 at a pharmacy in Boca Raton and $209.50 at a West Palm Beach pharmacy.

Times are tough. Drug companies say they need to make money to develop new drugs. They also need to make money to pay their CEOs huge salaries.

Pfizer, the company that developed Zoloft, the most widely prescribed antidepressant, paid its new CEO $12.6 million last year, even though earnings plunged. The former CEO walked away with an $82 million lump sum pension in 2006.

Among the problems I have with pricing schemes for mental health drugs, there is no "word-of-mouth" pressure to control the price. Shoppers gladly brag about the bargain they got on calcium supplements or complain about the cost of their blood-pressure prescription.

But who publicly prides themselves on the deal they got on this month's supply of the antipsychotic drug Seroquel or the steep price of Adderall?

No one. Because no one wants anyone to know they are on antidepressants, mood stabilizers, antipsychotic or schizophrenia drugs.

So, we pay what is asked without any questions. We assume we all pay the same.

The wide world of mental illness

One of the great things about the Internet - besides being able to shop 24/7 - is the global perspective it provides for free. I have created a Google alert that every week sends me articles about depression and mental illness from publications around the world.

I am often shocked and always grateful when I read these articles. As bad as treatment, stigma and misperceptions may be in the United States, they are much, much worse in other countries.

From an April 13 article in *The Times of India*: "A daughter suffering from a mental illness can be harrowing for an Indian father, for whom marriage is a social necessity. In fact, a large number of Indian families believe marriage to be a cure for mental illnesses like manic depression, bipolar affective disorders and even schizophrenia. The history of mental illness of the girl is therefore concealed.

"The illness then suddenly relapses because of discontinued medication. The girl is doomed. Neither her marriage works nor does she get cured. What parents don't realize is that they perpetuate the illness," one doctor said.

It's not so much about the cost of treatment in India. "It's actually about being answerable or accountable to the community," according to the article.

In Ghana, a study has found that the reason mental hospitals are crowded is because judges who send the mentally ill to hospitals until they are fit to stand trial "often do not follow up to continue with the judicial process, leaving the patients for unspecified periods of time in the overcrowded special ward of the hospital."

Doctors in Saudi Arabia have to deal with the superstition that mental illness is caused by the "evil eye" - which plagues those who envy the good fortune of others. According to a recent article in *Asharq Al-Awsat*, "the leading Arabic International Daily," stigma and superstition make it difficult to treat mental illness.

"For many, the prospect of being victims of the evil eye is far more convincing than the diagnosis of psychiatrists," according to the article.

Doctors who treat the mentally ill are often themselves portrayed as disturbed and the medicines they prescribe as addictive tranquilizers.

Back home in the United States, the new owners of a 19th-century mental institution in West Virginia have changed the hospital's name to the Trans-Allegheny Lunatic Asylum. According to the CBS News Web site, the new owners host tours, such as "The Nightmare Before Christmas." They are planning a dirt bike race called "Psycho Path."

It's a very small world.

Expectations: Premeditated disappointments

The night-blooming jasmine in my back yard is in bloom. My eyelids drop and I take a slow deep breath every time I walk by. It reminds me of my last major depression. When I was sick, sticking my face into a bloom of jasmine and breathing deep gave me a nano-second of peace when nothing in my world seemed good.

I planted the jasmine outside my bedroom after a two-month leave of absence that changed everything in my world.

Now that I am two years depression- and manic-free, I look back and - as weird as this may sound - I am actually grateful for that bout of despair.

I learned more in those months and made more changes in the last two years than I knew I was capable of or needed.

Codependency, anger, pride and self-inflicted martyrdom are toxic. But the biggest lesson I have learned is to get out of my own way.

I have caused a lot of my own grief by expecting my life to go a certain way. When people, places and things weren't going my way, I did what I could to force them back on my track. I had no spontaneity. And a life without spontaneity is a haven for mania and depression.

Getting well and staying well is as much about what I think and do as it is about my medications. There is a behavioral component to the mental illnesses I have.

Antidepressants and mood stabilizers will correct the physical problems. But I want long-term mental health. For that, I need to change the behaviors that create the physical problems. It is kind of like having high blood pressure: The medicine will stabilize it; changing your lifestyle will control it.

So, I am learning to wear my life like a loose-fitting linen shirt.

I love not planning. I love seeing what happens when I don't plan anything. I love living without a watch or expectations. I have learned the hard way that expectations are premeditated disappointments.

Yes, there are things in life I should plan: Protection from a hurricane, retirement, my daughter's college education, mammograms, teeth cleanings, birthday parties, even vacations - to a point.

But I do not - should not - plan every detail. Every expectation I dream up is an opportunity for disappointment.

Today, I am very careful about what I plan. The more control I exert, the more plans I make, the more chance for disappointment, frustration, resentment and jealousy - all are fuel for my depression.

Now, I devote every Sunday to spontaneity. I make no plans. I expect nothing. If something needs to be done, I do it during the week or on Saturday. Sunday morning I wake up, look at the ceiling and say, "Bring it on."

Then, I let life happen.

Woe is me

I had a fight with my sister a few years back. We covered a lot of ground. Looking back, I remember one thing she said to me. "You're such a victim. You always have to play the victim."

I was stunned. "What are you talking about?" I remember blurting out before I launched into a litany of my woes: I'm the single, working mom; I'm the one who checks the air in her tires and kills wayward rodents who slip past the dog; I pay all the bills, file the taxes and plan for retirement. Waaa ... waaa ... waaa ...

Of course, I didn't speak to her for the longest time. How dare she?

Today, I realize she was entirely right, and I couldn't entirely blame my Irish Catholic mother or the nuns at school for my martyrdom.

It was me. I had become St. Christine, patron saint of weary, underpaid and dateless single mothers everywhere. As twisted as it sounds, I kind of liked it.

My depression liked me that way, too. I lost track of time sitting alone at my kitchen table with a glass of wine and a laundry list of why I was entitled to whine. My imagination would fast-forward and fictionalize my resentments. When I finished the bottle, I was either crying or wanting to break something. I was free-falling - arms wide open - into my depression.

I cut out the wine, but I clung to my whining - always finding a reason why everyone should feel sorry for me and marvel at my unrelenting selflessness.

The sorrier you felt for me, the sorrier I felt for me, and all of that pity was like throwing gas on a burning fire.

I am nearly two years out from my last deep depression. I have devoted a lot of time to finding out about my illness and how to prevent another depression.

I have learned that the chemical balance we experience when we are in a depression skews the types of memories we are able to recall. When we are happy, we tend to think happy thoughts. When we are sad, we tend to think sad thoughts.

But today, I am not depressed. I can't use that as an excuse to sit on my pity pot. My medications are working well, and I now have confidence that my level, happy life is not temporary. Sad thoughts are optional. So, I have decided it is time to get to work on the other things that jeopardize my new life - like my martyrdom and victimhood.

Today, I have the ability to "think happy thoughts!" - which sounds silly and New Age-y. Still, it's true. When I catch myself focusing on a problem rather than the solution, I stop.

"OK, what's the solution?" I ask. And when I feel sorry for myself, I immediately try to think of someone or something that I am grateful for ... like my sister.

The "G" Word

Talking about God seems to make a lot of people uncomfortable. Mention God and a mental illness in the same sentence, and you might as well consider the conversation over.

It seems weird that a country founded by a bunch of folks who wanted religious freedom should wince when God is mentioned. But we do. So public discussions about treatments for mental illness rarely mention God, faith, spirituality or religion.

This, too, seems weird because many people who recover from a mental illness, or any illness, develop a profound belief or disbelief in a higher power.

For me, it was belief. Still, I don't discuss the part of my recovery and treatment for depression and bipolar with most people. I am afraid they will roll their eyes or twiddle their index finger beside their head.

I will blather on about the changes I have made in my diet, exercise and sleep regimens - even the dosage of my medications and side effects. I will tell you how wonderful I feel now, how I had no idea that a life could be a smooth pond rather than rolling breakers. But I won't mention God unless I know it is safe.

I want to change this. I will start now.

I was not a big God person before I got sick. Yes, I was raised a Catholic and occasionally went to Mass, but I did not consider God a buddy. Sure, I said my share of foxhole prayers and got down on my knees every day. But it was a punch-the-time-clock kind of relationship. Just wanted to make sure God knew that I knew he was on the job.

I read the Bible, as a historical document. I dabbled in the Bhagavad-Gita and found great inspiration in the teachings of the Buddha. I even tried to get through the Koran (but no one told me you have to read it from back to front.)

Then I did a swan dive into a black hole. The paradox of pain - emotional or physical - is that it opens your mind. Your pride and prejudices melt away. You become willing to try anything to feel better. I came to believe that I - alone - was powerless over my depression.

I needed medications from a doctor, friends to watch over faith and me that I would get better. I needed to accept that there is a power greater than myself and that I needed him/her/it. Thus began my relationship with my higher power, whom I call God.

This relationship is as important to my mental health as my medications and my family and friends. I know I risk getting sick again if I stop taking my medications, seeing my friends or praying and listening to God.

Meds, family, friends and God - not necessarily in that order.

Mental illness and potato chips: I can't have just one

I count. I will be walking the dog and notice that I am counting my footsteps. When I take the clothes off the clothesline I count the clothespins.

I do not do this consciously. I don't think, "Hey, how many steps is it to the dog park?" or "You should count the clothespins to make sure you have enough." I just start doing it. I know this is a symptom of obsessive-compulsive disorder but I am not like that Monk guy on television. Germs don't worry me, and I don't align my peas on my plate. By the time I count to 6 or 8 I stop myself.

My therapist also tells me that I am anorexic, although I think she is crazy. My body-mass index says I now am a healthy weight. But 18 months ago - in the midst of a deep depression - I will admit I was kind of thin. I always want to lose 5 pounds. I over-exercise, wouldn't dream of eating Häagen-Dazs and I weigh myself twice a day - at least. I have actually been overweight at times in my life but when depressed I stop eating.

I am telling you this because many people with mental illnesses such as depression and bipolar often suffer from a smorgasbord of other mental illnesses and disorders. Among mental health professionals it is called co-morbidity. Some anorexics are depressed. Some addicts and alcoholics are bipolar. Some schizophrenics have mood disorders.

Sometimes it feels as though you are one of those squishy toys. Squeeze one end and the other pops out. Squeeze the middle and the ends pop out. No matter what you do, is seem something is always popping out.

That's how it is with co-morbid mental disorders. You may get your depression under control but you still count clothespins. You manage your anxiety disorder but you are still a raging food addict. You quit drinking but you are still bipolar. Or you develop a completely new disorder!

Is it biological? Psychological? I will let the experts figure that out. For me, I work on recognizing when something pops out and remember that I am not weird or unique because I have other mental "issues." And it just doesn't matter how many steps it is to the dog park or how many clothespins are left.

Outing myself

I am open about my mental illness, and I am always fascinated by the responses I get when it comes up. The conversation usually begins when someone asks what I write about for the paper.

I explain that I have been writing for this paper for 22 years - most of those years covering criminal courts and the last 10 doing investigative reporting with data. I casually mention that I also write a weekly column on depression.

Then I hear several variations of "Oh":

The shotgun "Oh," as in, "Whoa, let's change the subject, quick"; The "Oh, really..." usually followed by their own or a loved one's heartbreaking experience with mental illness; and the wide-eyed "Oh," as if I just told them I was not wearing underwear or something.

Mostly I am shocked and saddened by how many people have personal experiences with mental illness.

Before I began writing about my own depression and mental-health issues in 2006, I had no idea so many people were touched by illnesses such as depression and bipolar. And I had no idea how people would react if I talked openly about it.

Now I know. Many, many times, it has enabled me to talk to people - and they to me - with a quiet kind of camaraderie.

People I have known for many years in many different capacities - people whom I never dreamed would ever speak to me of their personal lives - have shared. In those conversations, I witness a kind of honesty and humility that I have never seen.

There are those people, too, who have never spoken a word to me about my illness or my writing. I see them everyday. We nod, smile and walk by or make small talk about our kids or the weekend. I used to resent that. Today, I am OK with it.

Others have told me they just don't like what I write. I am OK with that, too. For me to judge their reactions is futile and wrong.

Because mental illness can be so hurtful, embarrassing and personal, I can understand why some people don't like to read about or discuss it. There are enough people judging those of us with mental illnesses; I don't need to judge them.

There are happy endings for many people with mental illness, although they rarely grab headlines. Trust me, Britney will not get the same ink when she is healthy again.

So, it is understandable that many people with mental illness choose not to go public.

I understand and respect that decision.

Today, 18 months after I began talking and writing about my depression, I wonder what my life would be like now had I not "outed" myself.

I believe I made the right decision. For me.

Progress in loss

Weimaraners are beautiful, hyper dogs. They have sleek gray coats, yellow eyes and are perhaps the most photogenic dogs since Lassie.

Until last week I owned one. No, I did not put her down. I could not provide the exercise and attention she needed so I gave her to my brother. On his 5-acre compound with his three Labradors, his family can give her everything a hunting dog could dream of.

This was a huge loss for me. Bella had been my constant companion during my depression. When I needed something with a heartbeat to hold, Bella was it. My desperation didn't frighten her and she became the shield between my fear and my daughter.

That dog got me out of bed. She wandered around the neighborhood with me on inky black nights when I could not sleep. She turned her head, every 10-15 seconds, to make sure I was OK. She was always there when I needed her, not telling me to pull myself up by my bootstraps and get over it.

I knew this was going to be sad. Real sad, with tears, long clingy hugs and endless second thoughts - the kind of stuff that can ignite a deep, ugly funk. I try to avoid funk-prone situations. They frighten me. This one was unavoidable.

The day before Bella left I busied myself with frantic yard work and dinner with a friend to avoid my feelings - destructive old behaviors that I have learned will only ratchet up my anxiety. Better to feel them and let them go than bury them inside. Yada, yada, yada ... therapy talk that has worked very well for me.

The next morning I took her to the dog park for one last run. It hit me, hard. I threw the ball over and over, tears streaming down my cheeks. She wandered around the park, turning her head every few yards to check on me.

Somehow I knew it was all going to be OK. Bella would be OK. I would be OK. I had a floor beneath me now. My feelings would not free-fall into my own private hell. Bella would be loved. I could handle all of this. I could not have a year ago. It would have crushed me.

There were more tears that day. I miss her. I will always miss her. I am still sad but I am not afraid of my sadness anymore. I do not have to manufacture some meaningless chore to divert my thoughts. I think about her. I get sad. It passes.

I think this is the way it is supposed to be.

Acting as if – or not

I was making dinner Monday night, half-watching the *NBC Nightly News*, when I heard anchor Brian Williams say something about suicide, smiles and the last week of January.

It sounded as though he had said something about a psychologist who found more suicides are committed in the last week of January. The psychologist's advice was to smile and say "hello" more often. I blinked hard. What? Did Brian Williams really say that? On national television? I got a transcript of the program and couldn't believe it. Indeed, the last week of January "traditionally sees more suicides."

"The reasons given? The holidays are over, the bills are coming in, the weather turns grim for many, and motivational levels are low," Williams said. "The psychologist's advice for staying above it ... Smiling at everybody you meet and saying 'hello' to complete strangers. That will at least get us to Tuesday."

As someone who has gone down the suicide road, turned around and come back, I do not believe that smiling at everybody and saying "hello" to complete strangers would have saved me. In fact, that kind of "acting as if" behavior would have masked my depression and prevented those around me from seeing how truly sick I was. I have heard of successful suicides that completely blindsided loved ones. No one suspected. "He seemed like everything was OK," they said. "Maybe a little down, but he seemed to be coming out of it."

I am not an advocate of feigning happiness - faking it till you make it. It seems emotionally dishonest. I don't believe that I could have smiled and "helloed" my way out of a suicidal depression. It might work for people suffering a credit-card hangover or failed-resolution blues, but probably not someone whose secret thoughts are of hoses and tailpipes and bullets and sleeping pills.

I was lucky. I had people in my life who could see through a forced smile or a fake "hello." They made me sign a contract promising not to end it. They checked on me. They didn't suggest I try to be chipper.

There are more than 32,000 suicides in the United States every year - about 90 a day. Most of these people gave some clue or warning, according to the National Alliance for Mental Illness. The signs may be obvious. Or they may be subtle.

Or they may be masked by a smile and a hello.

Public displays of emotion

Someone asked me what I thought of Hillary Clinton's tears when she was asked, "How do you do it?" during a campaign stop.

Forget about politics and sexism. This is another example of how utterly uncomfortable we are with feelings and emotions.

I don't care whether the pundits thought it was sincere or a red carpet-worthy performance. I want to know why, 36 years after candidate Ed Muskie shed a tear, we have made no progress - regressed, actually - in our attitudes toward expressing our emotions in public.

We still attach all kinds of silly and hurtful stigmas to our feelings: Crying means you are weak. Whatever you do, don't cry in public.

What is wrong with us?

Why do feelings make us so uncomfortable?

What does this have to do with depression?

Everything. Depression is an illness of feelings and emotions. A chemical imbalance in our brains thwarts our ability to regulate our emotions. We stay stuck in a feeling - not because we want to - but because our brains won't let us move on.

What a balding head or jaundiced skin are to cancer and liver disease, emotions are to depression.

When we are depressed, we lose the ability to "act as if" everything is fine. We cannot put on a happy face. Our feelings are not pretty and we portray them in their rawest: Desperation. Doubt. Disappointment. Defeat. Hopelessness. Humiliation. Rejection. Selfishness.

We cry a lot. When we hear others dissecting someone's tears - and judging them to be either justified, bad, weak or opportunistic - we isolate ourselves. If we drop a tear in public will you say the same things about us? We are ashamed of ourselves.

Actually, feelings and emotions are the body functions of our psyche.

They are neither good nor bad any more than sneezing or coughing is good or bad.

They are feelings.

They need to come out. We cannot always control when a sneeze or a cough will come upon us. It is the same with feelings. The best we can do is to learn to express them appropriately and not judge them in others.

If we judge, we encourage people to stuff down their feelings. That is not healthy. It is destructive, to ourselves and to those around us. It is emotional dishonesty. It can - and will - come out sideways and hit the innocent people around us. It can make us physically ill and trigger depression.

I will let the pundits pass judgment on whether Hillary's "weepy moment" - or the tearful displays of Ronald Reagan, Margaret Thatcher and Ellen DeGeneres - was genuine, warranted, sincere, staged, authentic, devious, heartfelt, manufactured, earnest, fake, spontaneous or contrived.

Maybe they just needed to cry.

Mental illness as entertainment

2007 was a big year for celebrities with mental illnesses.

Anna Nicole Smith died of an accidental drug overdose in February after allowing us - begging us - to sit in the front row and watch her illnesses humiliate her beyond belief on her reality TV show.

Paris Hilton, whose shallowness ran deep on her reality TV show, cracked with an undisclosed mental illness when sent to jail.

Lindsay Lohan and Britney Spears showed us raging alcoholism and addiction.

Owen Wilson proved that money, looks and celebrity don't protect against suicidal depression.

For comedian Richard Jeni, mental illness was fatal.

And does Angelina Jolie have anorexia?

I admit I watched the helicopter coverage of Paris Hilton's drive to jail and the ambulance pulling away from Owen Wilson's home. I even picked the long line at the grocery store checkout so I could read the tabloids. I am as guilty as anyone of rubbernecking at misery.

I don't feel good about this.

Are mental illnesses - depression, addiction, alcoholism and eating disorders - really entertainment? Should we be sitting on the edge of our couches waiting for the next episode on *E!* to show us what a celebrity looks like in the throes of an untreated illness? Would we watch a celebrity having an epileptic seizure?

We applaud celebrities who out themselves: Brooke Shields, Jane Pauley, Rosie O'Donnell, William Styron. We roll our eyes at celebrities who unintentionally out themselves after arrests or with their bizarre behavior: Mel Gibson, Margot Kidder, Courtney Love.

The argument can be made that seeing celebrities with mental illnesses raises our awareness. It proves that anyone can have depression or bipolar or addiction or alcoholism.

But does our obsession promote understanding, compassion and inquiry or are we sitting around gloating at their shame, embarrassment and self-abasement?

I don't know.

Holiday cocktail for depression

Here is the perfect cocktail for depression. Stress, financial insecurity, family gatherings, that *Feliz Navidad* song playing endlessly in your head ... and alcohol.

Welcome to the holidays. If you have depression you know you are just a few digs-from-the-in-laws away from losing it. Smothered by the goodwill and cheer we are supposed to feel, we sink. We drink. I used to take the edge off with spiked eggnog or champagne. I thought it would help me get that holiday spirit. It seemed to work for a few minutes. Then I plunged ever deeper and drank even more thinking it might make me feel better again.

I emerged from the New Year's holiday emotionally and physically hung-over. I beat up myself for the imminent bills and the 5 pounds I had gained. By February I was a wreck. Valentine's Day brought me to tears.

Then I learned that I had been fertilizing my depression with alcohol. I did not know that alcohol is a depressant. Yes, alcohol does blunt the effects of stress hormones, but only for a while.

Then it lowers serotonin and norepinephrine levels. Serotonin and norepinephrine are neurotransmitters that act as messengers, transmitting nerve impulses in the brain. Imbalances lead to depression.

Sure there are antidepressants that can restore the balance of these neurotransmitters. But if you are taking an antidepressant and you continue drinking, your antidepressant cannot do its job. You become more depressed, you have wasted a bunch of money and you will begin that endless cycle of trying to self-medicate your depression with alcohol.

Before you head out to the next holiday party, read the label on your antidepressant bottle. If it says, "do not drink alcohol," then don't. Remember, your in-laws will soon leave. You can lose that 5 pounds. However, if you slip into depression and can't work, those bills will not get paid.

Besides, there are a lot of benefits to not drinking over the holidays. You'll feel better. You'll sleep better. You'll have the patience to assemble complex toys. You'll have a trove of memorable embarrassing moments about your favorite relatives to share at

Holiday goal: Identify not compare

My Thanksgiving rush of gratitude is gone. I am locked and loaded in holiday-shopping mode. This brings financial insecurity, which leads to jealousy, then to resentment, pity and finally... depression.

I beat myself up for thinking that I should have more money so I can buy nicer gifts.

I covet the gifts in other shoppers' carts and the perfect Christmas they are going to have opening all those perfectly wrapped gifts while listening to Bing Crosby with their Hallmark families, perfectly posed in the portrait on their Christmas card.

Then, there are those hopelessly romantic, thoughtful, gorgeous guys bearing rocks in those blasted diamond commercials.

And how about those I'm-a-better-mommy-than-you magazines in the grocery checkout, with covers of a perfect three-story gingerbread house with curtains and a chimney that puffs powdered sugar smoke?

You see where I am going here? This is how depression thinks. This is the logic of a depressed mind.

Cigarette smoke can trigger an asthma attack, cold weather can aggravate arthritis and sick thinking fuels my depression. It's as if depression is an opportunistic virus just waiting for a chink in my immune system.

This year, things are going to change. Instead of focusing on what I don't have in common with people, I am going to look for what we do have in common during the holidays.

Even if it is just as simple as acknowledging that we both have eggnog in our shopping carts or that our feet hurt, although she is in Coach loafers and I am in Hush Puppies.

I am going to identify rather than compare:

"Don't these trees smell great?" instead of brooding over my little Charlie Brown tree and their 16-footer.

"It just doesn't seem like Christmas without snow," instead of "I bet you're leaving for Aspen on the 26th."

I haven't yet figured out how to identify with anyone on the diamond front.

I have spent a lot of time comparing myself to others. I am hard-wired to find our differences. It fuels my depression. It makes me feel "less than."

I slide into the victim role and isolate. If you have depression, isolation and loneliness are the enemy.

I don't think this will be difficult. When you think about it, we have a lot in common. I mean, aren't we all sick of that *Feliz Navidad* song by now?

Snapping the rubber band on negative thinking

I don't do disappointment well. I have gone through life assuming, actually expecting, the worst. It seemed the best way to protect my heart and feelings.

When things didn't go well, a little voice in my head would say, "Figures" or "Just my luck" or "What did you expect?" If something good happened, that little voice would say "Wow. Things like this never happen to me. It won't last."

I have done this with relationships, with jobs, with backed-up toilets and rained-out barbecues. I am an emotional Boy Scout, always ready to handle the worst. I have absolutely no idea how to handle "the best." Not a clue. I don't even know how to imagine the best, assume the best or hope for the best. Good results make me uncomfortable. Great results scare the hell out of me.

I can't imagine approaching a situation assuming that the best is inevitable, that things will surely go my way, that I will get what I want. Sure, it's always a possibility. But what are the chances of that happening, that sarcastic little voice asks.

This, I have learned, is fuel for my depression. I am always a few negative imperatives away from my black hole. This, I have been told, must stop. My therapist suggested wearing a rubber band around my wrist and snapping it every time a negative assumption popped into my head. I haven't done that. As often as I'd have to snap, I'm sure I'd have welts on my wrists.

Now that I am aware of this self-inflicted emotional sabotage, I see how it has poisoned my life. It has held me back and attracted negativity. It has whittled away at my self-esteem. I have deliberately lowered that bar on my wants and dreams to avoid disappointment.

The problem with this kind of revelation is that it makes me profoundly sad. It's like the clouds parted, and I can see that I have been holding the hand that holds me down - for years. I can see it in my teenage journals. Now, it has become incredibly frustrating to watch myself continue to do it.

I want to stop this. I want to assume the best will happen. I want to change the tape playing in my head.

The problem is I have no idea what that new tape should sound like. My therapist asked me what the new and improved voice would say. I shrugged my shoulders. I had no answer.

Until I figure that out, it may sound like the snap of a rubber band.

Loneliness, aging and depression

I had a friend who died of cancer last year. She was at least 30 years older than me. I never asked her age, to be honest. The last thing I remember her saying as she lay in bed, her room at hospice packed with friends and family, was, "This is heaven."

We told her she wasn't dead yet. "I know," she whispered. "I mean this is heaven."

She meant us. All of us. After her diagnosis, my friend made sure she was never alone. She hung out with women of all ages, joined our book club, went to parties and galas, and painted her fingernails purple. From the day of her diagnosis, she made a commitment to avoid depression and loneliness. She succeeded.

Loneliness among the elderly is tragic - and common. A recent study found that loneliness coupled with depression among the elderly is often fatal.

In the first-ever study of that topic, researchers in the Netherlands discovered that the mortality rate for people over 85 with depression and feelings of loneliness is twice that of those without depression or loneliness.

The problem is a lot of people think depression is part of the aging process. It is not. But because so many of us consider aging and depression natural, and some symptoms mimic the natural aging process, depression in the elderly is very often misdiagnosed and untreated.

An estimated 6.5 million of the 35 million Americans over 65 suffer from depression.

We think of teenagers when we hear about depression and suicide, but elderly white men have the highest suicide rate in the United States.

The causes of depression in the elderly are obvious: frustration with the loss of memory and physical ability, chronic pain or illness, moving into a nursing home, death of a loved one and financial insecurity.

The causes of loneliness in the elderly are also obvious, but for some reason, we tend to overlook them. A loss of hearing makes phone calls difficult. Trouble walking means no driving, no exercise and no pets. Vision problems mean no reading.

Most important, the elderly often are embarrassed and feel they can't tell anyone because someone might think they are losing their minds and need to be in a nursing home.

Imagine your life if you could not talk on the phone, go for a walk, drive to church or read a newspaper. Many of your loved ones may have died or moved away. Asking for help is not an option. Just imagine how lonely that would be.

The good news is that, once diagnosed, 80 percent of the elderly respond to medications and/or psychotherapy. The key is recognizing the signs of depression and finding help.

Among the symptoms to look for: memory problems and confusion, social withdrawal and loss of appetite, persistent and vague complaints, along with frequent calling and demanding behavior.

Dangerous objects, such as knives and guns, should be removed from the homes of older men with depression. Check on elderly family and neighbors, especially those living alone. Talk of suicide should be taken very seriously.

The thing to remember is that age does not have to be an obstacle to treating depression.

As my friend used to say, we just need a "shift in perception."

Codependency: Let me make you happy, please

When depression causes enough pain, you will reconsider options that once automatically raised your eyebrows: watching *Dr. Phil*, reading self-help books and rethinking your definition of psychobabble.

I did.

That's one of the few gifts of pain: You suddenly become less judgmental and more open-minded. For me, phrases like "feel your feelings," "inner child" and "codependency" became part of my vocabulary.

I am careful about using my new vocabulary around others. It seems wisecracks about depression treatments are really funny to some people. But my pride no longer blocks me from getting well.

Among my snicker-inducing efforts: a drum circle, meditation, yoga, reading Melody Beattie books, tracking down my inner child, and - my favorite - visiting a junkyard with a baseball bat.

None of this has been easy. By far the most difficult was learning about codependency and realizing that I am thoroughly, utterly and completely codependent. I have come to believe that nothing fuels my depression more than codependency.

There are a lot of definitions of codependency, and they cover a lot of behavioral ground. I have found author Melody Beattie's definition to be the easiest to understand: "A codependent person is one who has let another person's behavior affect him or her, and who is obsessed with controlling that person's behavior."

For us codependents, your emotional compass is our emotional compass. That means we can't be happy unless you are happy. If you are sad or angry, we will be sad or angry with you, even if it has nothing to do with us.

There is no emotional boundary between us. As the joke goes: A codependent wife wakes up in the morning, rolls over and asks her husband, "So, how do we feel today?" Funny, huh?

We think we are kind and considerate people, always thinking of others and what is in their best interest. Problem is, we are the ones defining what is in their "best interest." I have learned that people don't like that. Imagine?

We pick friends and spouses whom we think need our help and that we can control. Eventually, they rebel. Our feelings get hurt, and we get frustrated and sad, and we slide right into the martyr role, which is even more annoying.

Then we slide into the black hole.

I've spent a lot of time this year trying to define my responsibilities - not yours - and staying on my side of the street. Everyone is no longer entitled to my opinion. You can tell me your problems, and I won't try to solve them.

I will just listen and know that is enough.

Medication faux pas

I did something really, really stupid one morning last week.

I forgot that I had taken my meds and took them again. I got a double dose.

There was a time in my life when getting a double dose of certain drugs would not have bothered me. At all. Now, it scares the hell out of me.

I realized something was wrong when I got to work. A co-worker came over and we chatted. I told her I felt dizzy. My boss came over and asked about my weekend and how I was doing. I said I wasn't feeling right. Dizzy. Weird. Spacey. Thirty minutes later I couldn't focus. My typing looked like a 4-year-old's pecking at the keyboard. I left. I drove home - carefully - and called my nurse practitioner.

One of the medications didn't pose a problem, she said. The other did. She told me side effects to watch for and ordered me to bed. No problem. I slept until 3 p.m., woke up and wandered around the house the rest of the day.

In the 18 months I have been taking antidepressants I have never felt anything unusual or magical. I am sure this makes no sense to those of you who have never taken these drugs. They don't make me high. They are not "happy pills." I feel perfectly normal when I take these medications.

In time, you forget how potent they are. And maybe you forget to take them. Or you forget you've already taken them.

This hit me hard, maybe because I have tweaked everything in my life that I possibly can to prevent another major depression. I don't drink, smoke, take drugs, eat wheat or much sugar. I exercise. I meditate. I don't yell at the dogs. I notice any imbalance. And this was definitely an imbalance.

It can take years for a clinician to find the exact mix of drugs to balance a chemically imbalanced brain. For some, it never happens. For me, it had happened. I will never, ever again mess with that or take for granted how lucky I am.

I would like to blame this medicinal faux pas on the dogs whining for a walk at 5 a.m. or my oh-so incredibly busy and important life, or the pre-pre-pre menopause that seems to have set in.

I can't. This was my fault. Somewhere along the way I forgot how serious this disease is. I forgot how complex my brain is. I forgot how potent these drugs are. That is how I forgot that I had already taken my pills and ended up in bed with my two dogs and a scrambled brain.

Never, ever again.

Checking-up on my brain

Every three months - regardless of how I am feeling - I see my psychiatric nurse practitioner.

For her, this is standard operating procedure. For me, this is a new and foreign way of staying healthy.

Until I was diagnosed with depression, I went to the doctor only when my body was sick or broken. Sure, I do the routine mammogram, colonoscopy and teeth cleanings. But a three-month mental-health checkup seemed ... weird.

Still, I go. Yesterday was the day. I walked into her office, plopped onto her couch, and we began what would sound to most people like a Starbucks moment.

"So, how are you doing?" she asked.

I told her about my new dog. I bring her up to date on my daughter's sophomore year in high school. Her dog sauntered into her office. I scratched him and continued with my update: Guys, work, the ex, my vacation, what I've been doing for fun, blah, blah, blah ...

This is no trivial conversation. She watches me and takes notes. How am I sleeping? How is my appetite? More questions than a journalist would ask. She offers unsolicited advice that is always, and sometimes aggravatingly, correct.

I have learned that this is the way - the best and safest way - for me to be treated for a mental illness. Constant, seemingly eternal checkups.

These are not like the follow-up office visits I have made for physical ailments. Those visits focused on pain, range of movement, new test results, medication side effects, etc.

These mental-health checkups have introduced me to a new level of care. My checkups last at least 30 minutes. The nurse practitioner connects dots between mental and physical events that I would not have made. She tells me, insists, that now is not the time to mess with my medications despite having finally racked up some "happy" time and my hint that I would like to get off these drugs.

I know this is not the level of care that many people with depression receive. I know this because they are no better, often worse - and they usually stop taking their medications because they don't work. And for them, they really do not work. The brain is so complex. A drug that may work well for one, may not work at all for another.

There is no excuse when a mentally ill person - especially children and teens - suffer because a clinician is not following guidelines recommended by the U.S. Food and Drug Administration and the American Psychiatric Association. Those guidelines recommend weekly visits in routine cases to multiple times per week in more complex cases. Even more intense monitoring is recommended for children and teens.

Doctors should know this. The way I see it, if they don't know this, it's malpractice.

Dating and Depression

I got another dog. His name is ... Dog.

He is a mutt. Blond coat, black nose. One ear up. One ear down.

My friends cringed at the news. "Why?" "Really?" "Oh my God..."

I got Dog because my other dog, Bella - a high-strung Weimaraner - is, how shall I put it, "behaviorally challenged." I knew I had to do something when I came home from the gym and found a well-chewed biography of Carl Jung hanging from her mouth. I can take a hint. My vet said she needed a pal. She is lonely, he said.

Oh, was it this simple for us single folks with depression. These dogs already have a great, healthy relationship. They spent a few days setting their boundaries and divvying up the couch. Now, they hang out, doing nothing, just because they want to hang out and do nothing together. They are honest when they want to be alone. The other respects it. They don't ask what's wrong. They play. They fight. They never go to bed angry.

Watching them I realize that I, too, am "behaviorally challenged." I have always sought out behaviors that complement my depression. Even as a kid I was more comfortable alone. I began swimming competitively when I was 7. I could be with other kids but didn't have to talk to them and didn't have to worry that my clothes weren't good enough. The endorphin rush helped, too.

I never felt I fit in. My passions still are solitary endeavors. I read. I write. I exercise. I garden. I listen to music. I spend way too much time on the Internet. I walk on the beach. I spend as much time as possible on the bottom of the ocean.

When I drank, I drank alone. When I ran, I ran alone. I watch movies alone. I sleep alone. I don't like talking on the phone. Most of the time I don't mind being alone, which is exactly the company my depression seeks.

A lifetime like this has not given me the skills to form healthy relationships. I am divorced - twice. Dating is painful. My approach has always been the same: To figure out what would make him happy and then make him happy, even if he didn't agree with my definition of happiness for him. I figured if I could make him happy, then I would be happy.

It doesn't work that way. Controlling people has kept me stuck in my depression and unwilling to ask for help. It can be excruciatingly lonely and awkward.

I don't want to feel like this anymore. In the last few years I have really tried to break out of my solitude. I no longer "act as if" I am happy. I ask for help and let others help me. I (try to) respect others' boundaries.

And I will keep trying to find my genuine self and be it at all times. Just like these dogs.

A perpetual victim

It usually starts with resentment or a disappointment.

I roll it over, knead it and quietly let it rise.

Why did/didn't he tell me? Why did/didn't she do that? How could he? Why doesn't she? When will he?

Then a bunch of expletives. Then I raise my tired hand to my brow and become the patron saint of whiny, weary, single working mothers who have sacrificed oh-so-much and worked oh-so-hard and can't get a date, much less someone to walk the dog.

Yada, yada, yada. Woe is me. My soul flat-lines.

This is my "dysthemia," the low-grade depression that plagues so many of us with depression. Sometimes it seems worse than a major depression.

I hate it, especially now that I know I bring it on.

Before I began seeing a therapist and learning about depression, I would wallow in these feelings. As ugly and miserable as they felt, I had spent so much time as a victim and martyr that it had become my natural state of being. Normal.

Pretty sick, huh?

Then I heard something I did not like: Anytime I am angry or full of self-pity, it is my own fault. Stuff is going to happen or not happen. Deal with it. I thought this was pretty harsh, considering how mean and neglectful others had been to me. How could anyone say that to me?

Easy.

Here's the deal. I cannot control what others say or do. However, I can control how I react. Healthy people probably know this. But for some of us with depression, this is a startling, rude, revolutionary concept.

But true.

I have spent years - decades - unwittingly making myself sicker. I would let you push my buttons. When you were done pushing, I would hold them down myself.

Whose fault is that?

When people did or didn't do something I wanted/thought they should do, I would forget that expectations are premeditated disappointments and that it is not fair to expect people to run at my pace.

I have had to look at my role in perpetuating my dysthemia. Yes, there is a chemical imbalance. Yes the medicine helps. But changing my own behavior is just as powerful.

So, you can stop feeling sorry for me now. I threw my buttons in the trash.

A changed perspective

I got out of the shower this morning, walked into my bedroom and everything looked different but nothing had changed.

My damn dog - eternally loyal and infinitely stupid - was asleep on the bed. The hammock in the back yard was waiting, empty. The clothes on the clothesline were wetter than they were when I hung them because I forgot to take them down before it rained.

So what?

My 15-year-old daughter and I wear the same bikinis. The music blasting from her bedroom is the same music I listened to before school when I was her age, thanks to her current hippie phase. Being of that generation I know she is not using drugs.

Her boyfriend answers me with "yes, ma'am" and "no, ma'am" and I know this could be a complete ruse but I'm OK with it. I trust him. My child-support is on time. For now the bills are paid. I have a retirement account. Some days I love my job.

I look in the mirror and realize I have made peace with my gray hair and wrinkles and have come close to accepting the stretch marks.

My biggest problem is finding where the heck my daughter has put my makeup, and why - every single morning - does she have to use my makeup when she has a bag full of top-line cosmetics?

All these tangible things in my life have been exactly this way for a very long time. Yet in the deepest depths of my depression these same things made me weary. They were all a burden.

The dog always begged for a walk. The hammock was a taunting reminder that I didn't have time to relax. Laundry was endless. I worked to pay the mortgage. Writing was painful. Could you turn that music down? I look so old. Why bother with makeup? Damn the ex.

I am not achingly overwhelmed by these things anymore. I still get stressed, annoyed, worried, angry, sad and lonely.

Dealing with my depression, accepting it and constantly working on getting healthy has changed everything in my life. Everything. Maybe this is the way it is supposed to be. Maybe this is how life is when you don't have a mental illness. Or two or three mental illnesses.

Maybe I finally have a life.

All about meds

Never have so many had so much to say about the medicine we take. It seems that everyone has an opinion about antidepressants. Some want us to stop taking them. Others don't want to hear about them. Still others tell us how glad they are that we take them because we seem so much healthier.

To me, the most annoying are those who insist we stop taking our medications now. Some are friends, therapists and psychologists. Sometimes, it is a substance abuse counselor or sponsor. Sometimes - fed up with the weight gain or sexual dysfunction - we do it ourselves.

Listening to all these "suggestions" is tough and probably the No. 1 reason we don't tell people about our illness or medications. Not a week goes by that I don't hear a comment about antidepressants - some from people who know about my illness, others who spontaneously offer their expertise about a vast class of medications that saved my life.

You never hear people say, "You really should stop taking that blood pressure medicine" or "When are you going to quit that chemotherapy?" So why do some people feel so comfortable telling us what to do about our medications?

This is how I handle it. I listen. I let them say what they want. I understand that this is how some people offer support and show that they care about me. Then I make dang sure that I educate myself about my medications - the side effects, the dosage and exactly what the medicine is designed to do.

I ask myself: Am I comfortable with the doctor/nurse practitioner prescribing these drugs? What kind and how much training does this clinician have in treating mental illness? How much time did she spend on the examination? What questions were asked?

Did I walk out of the exam room understanding what I would be taking, why, what to expect, how soon to expect it and what to do if the medicine didn't work?

Did the doctor/nurse require a weekly follow-up call or visit when new medications were prescribed or dosages adjusted, as recommended by the American Psychiatric Association? Was therapy discussed? A change in lifestyle, diet or exercise?

Unfortunately, if you take antidepressants, you are going to have to deal with the stigma and ignorance still out there.

I learned the hard way that debating people - especially people who do not have depression or do not like antidepressants - is futile, frustrating and no fun. I let these folks offer their opinion, advice, suggestions, criticism and wisecracks. I say nothing.

This is between me, my therapist and the person writing the prescriptions.

Over-diagnosed or under-diagnosed?

Is depression over-diagnosed? Most likely, yes.

Why?

I believe it is because depression cannot be detected with a simple, cheap test.

Wouldn't it be great if you could go to the pharmacy and buy a little depression test kit, go home and wait for the stick to turn blue? Then we could go to our doctors, and they could confirm the diagnosis and prescribe the appropriate medicine.

A potentially fatal illness that cannot be confirmed with a test places physicians in an if-it-looks-like-a-duck legal and ethical quandary.

A patient comes in with all the symptoms of depression, so the doctor writes a prescription for an antidepressant.

Isn't it better - safer - to write a prescription than to find out that their patient's untreated depression landed them in a mental hospital or God forbid, the medical examiner's office?

People blame the pharmaceutical companies - everyone's favorite scapegoats - too. Boy, they've gotta love an illness that can't be easily diagnosed and has symptoms that mimic the blues, which every healthy human feels at some time.

With billions of dollars to be made, they hand out free samples and air commercials like that one with the heartbreakingly sad dog sitting by the door with a tennis ball in his mouth.

Then there are the drug addicts. Their Holy Grail is a long-term prescription that won't draw suspicion, preferably a benzodiazepine, such as Valium or Xanax. It's much easier to fake depression than chronic back pain.

We also have to consider the efficacy of these drugs. Since there are no tests, a doctor doesn't know the dopamine or serotonin levels of the patient.

That means that a doctor may have to prescribe a smorgasbord of antidepressants before finding the right one(s).

And, yes, there are doctors who just write the prescription because it's easy. There are pharmaceutical companies in the disease-mongering business. There are people who just want a little something to take the edge off every now and then.

Finally, though, there are people like us, who really have depression. Sometimes the over-prescribed-antidepressant debate really bothers me.

Then I remember that I don't want antidepressants - I need antidepressants. Thank God for my prescriptions.

Grief has no expiration date

I once wrote about a 15-year-old girl who was gang-raped on a beach during a romantic moonlight stroll with her boyfriend. She lost her virginity to three teenage rapists.

The girl had to tell her story to a courtroom full of strangers three times - at each of her attacker's trials. Four years later, an appellate court ordered new trials for two of the rapists. The girl - then 19 - had to come back to court to tell her story to a courtroom of strangers two more times. One of her attackers was convicted. One was acquitted.

At the sentencing hearing, she again described the fear, anguish and anger that still plagued her. The judge listened and imposed the maximum sentence - again. Then he told the girl he thought it was time she moved on with her life.

I was aghast. Grief - whether it is over the loss of your virginity to rapists or the loss of your wife of many years - has no expiration date. Grief should be respected. No one but the grieving person has the right to decide when the grieving is over.

That's not to say that friends and loved ones should ignore it, avoid it or be afraid to offer help, suggestions and encouragement, especially when the grief turns into depression.

This kind of grief can cause adjustment disorder, also called "situational" depression. It does not necessarily mean that the person has a lifetime diagnosis of depression. But it is depression nonetheless, and a person in depression should not be told to pull themselves up by their bootstraps and move on.

My suggestion: Offer empathy and your ear. Understand that there are five stages to grief: anger, denial, bargaining, despair and, finally, acceptance. Ask yourself: "Is what I am saying and doing helping them go through each stage? Or am I judging the pace of their grief?"

My parents were terminally ill seven years ago. My father died first. Sixteen months later, my mother died. I learned that you must do all five stages before you can pass "Go." I did not. I plowed ahead, thinking the worst was over when we buried my mom. It wasn't. Every time a strong feeling surfaced, I stuffed it down. Then, they started coming out sideways. Finally, I went in a deep depression.

You don't have to do these stages in any order. Some you do during the tragedy. Some come later. You may do a stage once. You may do it over and over until it is over. You may have to take antidepressants. That is OK. Antidepressants won't insulate you from grief. They will, in my experience, give you a floor on which to stand so you can get through each stage without sliding into a deep, dark hole.

Grief is not a race. The more willing I was to go through these stages, the faster I healed. The more support I accepted - from prayers, friends, therapy and antidepressants - the more I wanted to heal.

Today, I run at my own emotional pace.

Keeping good company

We - those of us with depression and bipolar - are not alone.

Actually, we are in some very good company:

Art Buchwald, Sigmund Freud, Marilyn Monroe, Ted Turner, Greg Louganis, Alanis Morissette, Lionel Aldridge (three-time Super Bowl winner and sports broadcaster), Abraham Lincoln, Leo Tolstoy, Mike Wallace, Georgia O'Keeffe, Roseanne, Sir Isaac Newton, Franz Kafka, Jean-Claude Van Damme, Carrie Fisher, Tipper Gore, Jackson Pollock, Barbara Bush, Kitty Dukakis, Congresswoman Lynn Rivers, D-Mich., Phil Graham (owner of *The Washington Post*), Abbie Hoffman, Robert

McFarland (former national security advisor), Winston Churchill, Ilie Nastase (tennis player), Jimmy Piersall (baseball player and broadcaster), Buzz Adrin, Stephen Hawking, Salvador Luria (Nobel Prize winner/ bacterial genetics), Francis Ford Coppola, Patty Duke, Alvin Ailey, Dick Clark, Drew Barrymore, William Faulkner, F. Scott Fitzgerald, Ernest Hemingway, Joseph Conrad, Eugene O'Neill, Tennessee Williams, Virginia Woolf, Irving Berlin, Axl Rose, Cole Porter, Sarah McLachlan, Eric Clapton, Kurt Cobain, Hector Berlioz, Sting, Robert Schumann, Sheryl Crow, Ray Charles, Brian Wilson, Tom Waits, T.S. Eliot, Sylvia Plath, Walt Whitman, Vincent van Gogh, Mark Rothko, Michelangelo, Edvard Munch, Thomas Jefferson, Robert Downey Jr., Dick Cavett, Spalding Gray, Vivien Leigh, Margot Kidder, Mariette Hartley, Ben Stiller, Jonathan Winters, Larry Flynt, Congressman Patrick Kennedy, William Styron, Danny Bonaduce, Bobby Brown, Rosemary Clooney, Connie Francis, Graham Greene, Phil Ochs, Tony Orlando, Darryl Strawberry, Phil Spector, Noah Wylie, Naomi Judd, Ludwig Van Beethoven, Frederic Chopin, Truman Capote, Emily Dickinson, Edgar Allan Poe, Jim Carrey, Jane Pauley, Lorraine Bracco, Brooke Shields, Amy Tan, Anne Rice, Billy Joel, Billy Corgan (Smashing Pumpkins), Adam Ant, Robin Williams, Drew Carey, Mandy Moore, Rosie O'Donnell, Uma Thurman, Harrison Ford, Terry Bradshaw, Trent Reznor (Nine Inch Nails), Boris Yeltsin, John Denver, Marie Osmond, Princess Diana, Rodney Dangerfield, Joan Rivers, John Kenneth Galbraith, Napoleon Bonaparte, Agatha Christie, Cary Grant, Victor Hugo, Mark Twain, Mozart, Cara Kahn (MTV's *Real World*), Aristotle, Francesco Scavullo (photographer), Elizabeth Taylor, Anne Hathaway, Charlie Pride, Evan Dando (Lemonheads), Robin Williams, Thelonious Monk.

And you. And me.

Life without an OFF switch

I have been diagnosed with a type of bipolar called hypomania. I am going to try to explain what it feels like to be bipolar - a form of depression characterized by severe mood swings.

When I am manic, I feel like a racehorse in the gate, waiting for the bell. Sitting still for a hair appointment is almost impossible - one of the reasons I have let my hair go gray, or "silver," as I like to say. My thoughts race. If I do become fixated on one thought, it consumes me. I become obsessed with thinking through every detail, possibility and outcome. This has made me a successful journalist.

Let me give you an example. I was once assigned to cover the case of a young man who walked into his parents' bedroom and shot them as they slept. The father died. The mother lived.

Within moments of hearing the news, I had analyzed the entire case. Would the kid's attorney ask a judge for a furlough so he could attend his father's funeral? Would the Department of Corrections allow the mother (the victim) on the visitor list of her son (the killer)? And would prosecutors subpoena the mother and force her to testify against her only child - testimony that could put him in the electric chair?

Today, I analyze data for investigative projects. I can sit in front of my computer for hours, unaware of the time - amped on trying to find an answer.

Then there are the physical symptoms. My muscles ache to be used. I exercise until my heart rate reaches 180 beats per minute. My off switch doesn't work. I once ran the last 5 miles of a marathon without shoes because they hurt my feet.

But when I am down, I want to be alone. Caller ID is my best friend. I don't talk much. I do my work and try to look so busy that no one will bother me. I am not tired. I am weary. Life is bleak. Numb days roll by. I have no hope that life will get better.

In between, there can be long periods of feeling stable and content. Life is fine, except I'm waiting...

Today, the anxious ache that once welled up every time I inhaled is gone. With the help of my therapist, my nurse practitioner and my medications, I now have an emotional floor beneath me. Sadness and anxiety have expiration dates. I can pause when agitated. I understand that everyone is not entitled to my opinion.

I have serenity.

If you are not bipolar, I cannot describe how wonderful and amazing this feels - believing that you can trust your ability to handle your feelings and that you won't lose these skills.

Life can be good.

Happy pills are not funny

Twice in the past week, I heard antidepressants being called "happy pills." I do not like this. I take antidepressants. I do not take "happy pills."

When you make a wisecrack about my medicine, I hear you saying that you don't take depression - or antidepressants - seriously.

First, let me say that antidepressants don't make you happy. Ecstasy is a happy pill. Maybe even Viagra. Antidepressants are not happy pills. I do not get high off my antidepressants.

I like the way antidepressants are described on www.depression-guide.com: "They are not happy pills; they don't artificially induce a feeling of bliss or unrealistic well-being. No medication can do that, except for alcohol and some illegal drugs, and their effects don't last. Nor do antidepressants insulate you from life, make you not care about important things, or insensitive to pain or loss. Tranquilizers can do that, for a while, but antidepressants can't."

Here is what antidepressants do: "All antidepressant medications work by influencing the activity of neurotransmitters in the brain. ... Antidepressant medications work by slowing the breakdown of neurotransmitters and enhancing the sensitivity of receptors on the receiving neurons."

I know when I make a stink about "happy pill" jokes, people roll their eyes behind my back. They say I'm too sensitive. "Come on, it was just a joke. You need to lighten up. Can't you take a joke?"

Not funny.

One of the biggest obstacles to seeking treatment for depression is stigma - especially for men. Depression is widely viewed as a namby-pamby pseudo-illness. "It's a great way to get time off from work!" "They're not really sick, they're just faking it!"

When you say stuff like that, people stay in the closet. They don't talk about their disease. And talking about your disease with others who suffer from the same disease has proven to be very, very helpful.

My parents, who had cancer, made great friends and found enormous comfort in their cancer support group. There are support groups for people with HIV, cystic fibrosis, eating disorders, diabetes and Down syndrome. Thank God there are a few mental health self-help groups, like Recovery Inc. But most physicians haven't heard of this 70-year-old self-help group, much less know where and when its meetings are held.

Another problem with the "happy pill" joke is that recovering addicts and alcoholics who also suffer from depression and bipolar - and about half of them do - won't, or feel they can't, take them because a "happy pill" will make them high. And then they relapse. Just ask anyone in the treatment industry: Untreated depression and bipolar is probably the No. 1 cause of relapse.

This is why "happy pill" is not funny to us. We are not faking it. We are not taking "happy pills." We are trying to get well. It's no joke.

Feeling bad or feeling you are bad?

A very wise woman taught me the difference between guilt and shame. Having been brought up Catholic I just kind of figured they were the same and would be as persistent in my life as bad hair days.

I was wrong, she told me. Guilt, she said, is the feeling you get when you have done something wrong. Guilt is a good thing. It is what separates us from the Ted Bundys of the world.

My guilt hits me in the sternum. I know it's real when it passes my "Guilt Validity Test" - how many times I rehash, justify or rehearse an explanation for something I have said or done.

If the voice in my head starts sounding like District Attorney Jack McCoy on *Law & Order*, I'm guilty. I say a prayer, make amends and let it go.

Shame, my friend said, is an inherent feeling that you are bad. It doesn't hit any specific place in the body. It is the essence of your soul, and if you have depression, it's like a perpetually burning pilot light that keeps those rotten feelings nice and cozy.

Shame can happen when a child is abused or neglected and blames herself for what happened to her. She must have been a bad girl for someone to do that to her or to have abandoned her. Right?

Sometimes shame happens with the best of intentions, when a parent or teacher or religion teaches us that we must perpetually watch our moral compass because if we don't, we won't be saved. Keep being bad and you will end up in H-E-Double-Hockey-Sticks, mister.

Shame, my friend said, serves no purpose. It will make your depression much, much worse. It will make getting better almost impossible, regardless of the medications and therapy.

As your depression gets worse, the shame seeps in and convinces you that because you feel bad, you must be bad. Then it shreds your self-esteem.

The worse you feel about yourself, the less you can help yourself and others, she said. You can and probably will pass that shame on to your children as unwittingly as you may give them the family depression gene, she said.

And this I will not do.

Happiness 101

Lately, I have been thinking about happiness. Not the kind of happiness you get when your teenager spontaneously empties the dishwasher or Nordstrom has a great sale.

I mean long-term, sustained happiness. Maybe even that perpetual state of bliss called "enlightenment" that the Dalai Lama talks about.

If you are like me, and you suffer from depression, you would probably settle for 40-watt enlightenment, because the notion of long-term, continuous happiness or even contentment is foreign.

If you don't have depression or bipolar, this might sound stupid. But I have spent a lot of time waiting for something bad to happen. Or assumed I would spend my entire life bouncing from one dilemma to the next - so why bother?

Now that my medications are stable and I've been seriously working on "my issues" - as they say - I'm wondering whether I might be a candidate for lifelong happiness.

So I went to the library and found the Dalai Lama's *The Art of Happiness* on CD. I listened to this when it came out in 1998 and thought it was pretty groovy, then forgot everything his holiness had said.

I checked it out of the library and began listening to it from the perspective of someone who is well trained at prolonged un-enlightenment. I got to Chapter 4 on the CD and surrendered. The Dalai Lama was moving too fast for me. I couldn't keep up with all the happiness suggestions.

I decided to do it the old-fashioned way. I got the book, a yellow highlighter and approached it as a student. Right away, bad news: "Although it is possible to achieve happiness, happiness is not a simple thing."

Buddhists believe there are "four factors" of happiness: wealth, worldly satisfaction, spirituality, and enlightenment. Yikes. I have a lot of work to do.

This is OK. I don't mind. At least I have some kind of blueprint.

I need this because when you live with depression, you acquire behaviors and ways of thinking that feed the disease. They become routine, then instinctive. You react to things, you make choices that say, "There's something wrong with me," and "I don't deserve anything better" and "I'm not worth it," and "I'm sorry, I know I'm not much fun to be around."

That's why I need a therapist - to help me recognize and unlearn this stuff. That's why I need someone to show me the blueprint. I need steps to follow. I need directions.

Because I really think I can do this now.

My weight, my depression

You can tell the state of my mental health by my weight.

I am nearly 20 pounds lighter than I was 18 months ago, when I first slipped into a major clinical depression.

At its worst, I simply forgot to eat because the depression switched off my hunger button. My stomach would growl and growl, but its connection to my mouth was gone.

Today I think I look good. I've gained back a few pounds and my friends tell me I look better than last year, when my clothes hung loose and I had no desire to shop - another sure sign of a my state of mind.

I feel good, too.

But my therapist still is on me like the morning dew about my weight. She used to make me write down everything I ate. A co-worker just asked, "What do you weigh now, like, 10 pounds?"

Depression and antidepressants can cause weight gain or loss. I can look back at my life - and envision the number on the scale - and see exactly when I was depressed.

Losing or gaining that kind of weight without deliberately changing your diet isn't normal or healthy. I now know that when that happens, I need to get help - immediately.

I consider myself lucky, though. I'm taking a medication that makes me want to eat fruit. Vast quantities of fruit, especially pineapple. (This was not mentioned as a side effect on the label.) Sometimes, to get better, you have to take medicine that will pack on the pounds. I know a guy who suffers from bipolar disorder who gained nearly 40 pounds after beginning his medication.

Imagine feeling your absolute worst, your self-esteem below zero and your doctor says the medicine you need is going to up your dress size into the serious double-digits. For depressed women, in particular, this can be devastating.

We can't walk through a checkout line at the grocery store without wondering whether the pin-thin models could fly if they flapped those protruding wing bones fast enough.

How is gaining 40 pounds going to make anyone feel better? I don't know. I'm not going to be trite and profess that we shouldn't be so conscious about our body image. I have tremendous empathy and respect for these people and their effort to go to any lengths to get better.

As for me, I've added my scale to my anti-depression toolbox, which also contains my medications, my friends' phone numbers and a really great pair of patent leather ruby red Stuart Weitzman stilettos - still in the box.

The upside of menopause

Good news! Come to find out, antidepressants actually minimize the effects of menopause. Not that I'm actually in menopause, or even that close (depending on your definition of close. I define close as 10 minutes.)

Still, there is an upside to depression if you're in (near) menopause and take antidepressants. That's the word from my gynecologist, who was explaining this to me during my annual exam.

When I told her what I was taking, she asked how I felt. "Better than ever," I told her. I feel so good, I don't even have PMS anymore, which will come as stunning news to a couple of my exes.

Anyway, it's true what they say about antidepressants and menopause, and there's research to prove it.

Clinical trials have shown that a class of antidepressants called selective serotonin reuptake inhibitors can relieve symptoms of menopause. According to the Mayo Clinic's Web site: "Many doctors now consider these antidepressants the treatment of choice if you can't - or choose not to - take hormone therapy."

Estrogen replacement has traditionally been the treatment for menopause symptoms. But women with heart or liver disease, and women with problems with blood clots and certain cancers shouldn't take hormones, according to the U.S. Department of Health & Human Service.

And so we have choices: hormone therapy, alternatives such as herbs, antidepressants and mood stabilizers, or nothing at all. My mother toughed out her menopause without any hormones or other treatment. I don't know how she did it, especially considering she worked full-time and had three kids in college. Yikes.

I have a friend who is smack in the middle of her menopause. She swears she either has to be on hormones or antidepressants, or else.

An estimated 1.3 million women hit menopause every year. But we women who have a history of depression before menopause must be really vigilant. Studies have shown that we are the women most likely to suffer a major depression during "the change."

So here we go, my depressed lady friends. Looks like we can stand together at the edge of that big black hole with our Botoxed foreheads, chin hair, tweezers, jiggly triceps ... and know that what we have already been through and what we have done to take care of ourselves might stop us from jumping in.

Medicating the mother-to-be

I have a friend who just found out she is pregnant. She is due in November. It is their first child and she and her husband are thrilled.

But there is the matter of her antidepressants. Should she continue taking them while pregnant? This dilemma never crossed my mind, seeing as my childbearing years are basically over unless there is another virgin birth and this anti-aging cream actually does turn back the hands of time.

So, I asked my younger friends in their childbearing years who struggle with depression what they thought. It's a hot topic. One friend told me that her sister has a long history of depression. When she got pregnant her doctor insisted that she stop taking her antidepressants and she did. While pregnant with her first child - what should be one of the happiest most exciting times in a woman's life - she sunk into a deep depression and stayed there for months. She was too depressed to nurse.

There used to be a belief that the torrent of hormones that rush through us during pregnancy would protect us from depression. Research has shown that isn't true. A study funded by the National Institute of Mental Health found that pregnant women who stop taking their antidepressants "may significantly increase their risk of relapse during pregnancy."

"The study demonstrated that pregnancy itself is not protective," according to an NIMH press release issued in February 2006. Of the pregnant women in the study who stopped taking antidepressants, 68 percent relapsed. But of the pregnant women who kept taking their antidepressants, only 26 percent relapsed.

If there is one thing a pregnant woman does not need it's another reason to become depressed. We spend weeks throwing up, followed by double digit weight gain and stretch marks. But wait! There's more. Swollen ankles, hair loss, backaches and seemingly endless weeks of a boulder on your bladder. I cannot even imagine throwing depression on top of this.

But add to this load these warnings:

"Women of childbearing age should be aware that lithium increases the risk of congenital malformations in babies. Special caution should be taken during the first 3 months of pregnancy," according to the NIMH Web site.

And this: "Some researchers have found that depression during pregnancy can raise the risk of delivering an underweight baby or a premature infant," from the U.S. Department of Health and Human Services Web site.

"Some women with depression have difficulty caring for themselves during pregnancy. They may have trouble eating and won't gain enough weight during the pregnancy; have trouble sleeping; may miss prenatal visits; may not follow medical instructions; have a poor diet; or may use harmful substances, like tobacco, alcohol, or illegal drugs."

I do not know what I would do if faced with this decision. But I do know I would be honest with my obstetrician and ask for help from my friends and family. And I might buy that sign I once saw at a Cracker Barrel restaurant.

"If momma ain't happy, nobody's happy."

Dual-diagnosed and damned

The people I know in recovery have peculiar ideas about antidepressants. I have heard recovering alcoholics say, "I've managed to stay sober for X number of years without having to take mind-altering drugs" - referring to antidepressants and mood stabilizers.

They say it like it's something to be proud of, like they are better than the addict or alcoholic who also suffers with another potentially fatal mental illness - depression - and takes medication to control that disease. To me, that kind of proclamation sounds about as rational as a diabetic saying, "I've managed to stay alive for X number of years without having to take insulin."

Why are the dual-diagnosed - those with addiction and depression - stigmatized even within their own? Does the recovery community not understand that a recovering alcoholic gets no more of a buzz from an appropriately prescribed antidepressant than a diabetic gets from insulin?

Apparently not. I know of a dedicated drug treatment counselor who worked for years at a respected rehab center. When her bosses found out she was on antidepressants they told her she would have to quit or stop taking the drugs. She stopped taking her antidepressants. Then she killed herself.

Studies have shown that at least one-third of alcoholics and half of addicts also suffer from another mental illness, such as depression or bipolar disorder. So, why do the lucky ones look down on the dual-diagnosed, telling them they're not really clean and sober as long as they're taking these "mind altering" antidepressants?

I know many addicts have extensive experience in pharmacology. But should an addict who might never have taken a legal drug in an appropriate dose criticize other recovering addicts and alcoholics who are taking appropriately prescribed antidepressants? I also have heard those in recovery talk openly about their fear of using pain medications after surgery.

But rarely will a recovering addict or alcoholic admit to taking antidepressants. That means the dual-diagnosed cannot fully participate in a 12-step program - the most successful treatment for addiction - without worrying about being judged by their luckier peers, who don't have both illnesses.

Why should we care? Because an estimated 17 million Americans are addicted to drugs or alcohol - more than 7 percent of the population.

It is said that every alcoholic or addict has a profound impact on the lives of at least five people - perhaps their parents, siblings, children, spouse or other family members, a friend or a boss.

You don't need to do that math if you are among those five people. You just need that addict or alcoholic to get help - all the help - they can get.

Teenage journals: Remembering a lifetime of depression

Last week a thief smashed my car window and stole my purse. Along with two new lipsticks, my favorite faux zebra-skin wallet with pink trim and a really nice purse I had bought six months earlier in New York, I lost all my identification: Three credit cards, one checkbook, my driver license, insurance cards, press pass, sunglasses and my cell phone.

After a few not-so-ladylike expletives and a couple of woe-is-me minutes sitting on the curb waiting for the police, I decided to get off my pity pot and get a grip. Things like this happen. I cancelled the credit cards, my cell phone and my bank account. Since I pay all my bills electronically, this meant contacting each company and authorizing them to pay my bills from my new bank account number

That's when I started the hunt for my most recent electric bill. I looked everywhere. Couldn't find it. Finally, I pulled down an old file box on the shelf in my closet. I didn't find the bill. But I did find the journals I had written as a teenager.

I don't have many memories of my teenage years. I can't remember most of my teachers. I couldn't tell you the principal's name. The faces in my yearbook look so familiar but I can't remember much about any of them. I have even fewer memories of my childhood.

I now know why. I was an extremely depressed - and suicidal - teenager. One journal entry begins "Why can't dying be as easy as living?" It ends "Just let me expire..."

My therapist, who has been bugging me for months to dig out these journals, listened. Wide eyed, she proclaimed, "You were clinically depressed as a teenager."

I always knew something was wrong. My mother used to say, "I know you're unhappy. Things will be better after you graduate." Sometimes things would get better. Then I would fall into another black hole. Isolate myself, blare The Who's *Quadrophenia*, write about boys and the teenage wasteland I inhabited.

This is why I buried the journals in a box on the shelf in my closet, so high up that I needed to stand on a chair to get at them. Once, about 10 years ago, I tried to read them. After a couple of sad pages I vowed never to read them again or to ever keep a journal.

I gave them all to my therapist.

Then I cried. I have had this illness for over 30 years. A lifetime. I wasn't always in my black hole. There were very good times. But always there was this underlying melancholy and a feeling like the good times couldn't last. Like I was always waiting for something to happen.

I cried for the lost years. I cried because in those journals I felt again the pain of a depressed teenager, a more visceral and despondent pain than the depression of a weary 40-something single mother who can't see beyond the bills, the dirty clothes, the full dishwasher and the exasperating question: "What's for dinner?"

I cried because there are still countless teenagers out there who don't know that they're sick. All they know is that there is something wrong with them, that they are different. The other kids don't like them. Life will never change, never get better. They will never fit in. They will never be happy. They will always be miserable and alone.

I cried because it shouldn't have taken 30 years to find out this isn't true.

Ignorant of injustice

Since I graduated from college many, many years ago (the exact number isn't important) I have been fortunate - blessed - with jobs that offer medical insurance. Over these many, many years (again, the exact number isn't important), I have developed this Pollyanna attitude toward medical care. I get sick. I go to the doctor. I whip out my insurance card, and my portion of the bill is magically reduced, usually 80 percent.

Best of all, I have this amazing prescription drug program. If you are prescribed maintenance medications, such as antidepressants and mood stabilizers, you fill out a form, put it in a postage-paid envelope along with your prescription and credit-card number. A few days later the mail carrier delivers three months' worth of the drug for $40. Any drug, three months, $40.

So, I have recovered from a major depression in blissful ignorance about the actual cost of my therapy, office visits and prescriptions, until a couple of weeks ago. For some reason, I read all the fine print, curious about where the heck these drugs come from and why they all cost $40. And there it was - the actual cost of three months worth of my prescriptions: $886.61. I did the math. If I didn't have insurance, it would cost me $3,546.44 a year to buy my medications. I was stunned and embarrassed at my ignorant and pretentious attitude about access to and the cost of prescriptions and health care.

The pharmacist at my grocery store said some people can only afford to buy a few pills at a time. I have a friend who makes only $18,000 a year, but that is too much to qualify for free health care. If the cost of his medications was deducted from his income, he would easily qualify. He survives on free samples from his psychiatrist.

I have another friend who just turned 62. She works, but her income is so modest that she still qualifies for free care from the county health-care district. She just got her first Social Security check, and now her income is too high. Her prescription and health- care coverage will be cut off. She has no idea what she will do.

Everyone knows about the prescription drug crisis in America. Those who need a prescription and can't afford it suffer. Some die. But when mentally ill people don't get their medications, really bad things can happen. Many medicate with drugs and alcohol. Some become homeless. Some become criminals. Many become victims.

Our jails, our prisons and our hospitals have become the primary mental-health caregivers in our country - providing just enough care and medication to ship them out without any follow-up care. The cost is staggering.

Wouldn't it be cheaper to pay for their care and medication than to pay for the prosecutors, judges, public defenders, emergency-room nurses and doctors, prison guards, probation officers and foster parents needed when they can't afford care and medication?

All this because someone who isn't as fortunate as me can't come up with thousands of dollars to pay for the same drug that costs me - the lucky one - just a few hundred dollars a year.

Delivered to my door.

Social anorexia

I used to think that I was only afraid - really afraid - of cancer, sharks and car wrecks that require the Jaws of Life to get you out.

Now I have a new fear: sinking into another major depression. I am flat-out terrified of sliding down to the bottom of that block hole again. It was a year ago last Tuesday that I left work telling myself I could not go on. Alternating between catatonic and sobbing. Unable to read or write or eat.

I will do anything to avoid another black hole - anything. And so I created this safe little world. My work - with a boss who gently reels me in when I'm too up or down. My posse of girlfriends and my daughter - who make sure I eat enough. My home - a serene little sanctuary. Walking the dog, working out at the gym and watching reruns of *Law & Order*.

I didn't used to be like this. Once, as a reporter, I nearly walked into crossfire in a nasty part of town. When people hung up on me during a testy interview I would wait a minute, call them back and coyly explain that we must have been cut off. I got knocked down by an aggressive cameraman when I was 4 months pregnant, wrangling to get in front of a pack of paparazzi. I witnessed an execution. I scuba dived. I mountain biked. I liked to ride on the back of motorcycles.

But now my life is very safe. I don't take risks. I don't like controversy or excitement. Nothing will hurt me. Except that nasty phone call with my ex last week that took me from zero to hoses and tailpipes faster than I could call a girlfriend.

A box of Kleenex later, I vowed to build a wall around my world.

A psychologist told me this is social anorexia and it is not uncommon among those who recently recovered from a major depression. But in order to fully recovery, I must get back to taking the risks that make life thrilling and accomplished.

My therapist and girlfriends saw this and told me I didn't need a phone call. I needed a date. Just hop on the Internet, they said, and at least take a look. Just do what you like to do and you'll find a guy who likes doing the same thing, my therapist said.

I like volunteering. I took a commitment at a local mental hospital every other Saturday night. I like it except the guys I meet can't wear shoelaces. And Saturday night, my therapist pointed out, is date night. So find another volunteer gig on another night, she said.

This seems like a lot of work - dating and relationships - for something with the pain potential of a chain saw ripping through your heart. But if I'm going to learn to live with depression, I need to stop starving my free spirit. I've got to learn to live with fears and chain saws. That scares me.

The depressing truth

My antidepressants sit on the counter beside my coffee maker. There is more than one bottle. Most of the time I don't notice them. They are as welcome on my counter as the cutting board and the dog's cookie jar. They are as much a part of my routine as my first cup of coffee.

But sometimes I do notice them. They weren't there a year ago. They remind me of what I was like. Then I begin with the "what ifs" and "maybes."

It sounds something like this: What if I hadn't been so bullheaded and had admitted years ago that I needed help? What if I hadn't dug my nails so deep into that marriage/relationship/job, thinking that if I just worked a few more hours, if I could just keep the house cleaner, if I could lose 10 pounds, if I could make someone happy, I might feel better? What if my husband/boyfriend/boss could see me now? What if I could have seen how much my illness hurt me and those I love? Maybe my marriage/that relationship/that job would have lasted...

These thoughts have been part of my recovery from depression. It's like the clouds parted and now I can see how miserable I was and was to be around. I use these thoughts to beat myself up. When I beat myself up, I start feeling depressed all over again.

So, what good are these thoughts? Can these "what ifs" and "maybes" keep me healthy?

Yes. I have found they can. They have taught me humility and acceptance. I have had to accept that I have this illness. I had to accept that I need those pills next to my coffee maker. I had to accept that I hurt others and myself. I have to accept that I cannot change the past.

Those little pills have given me more than happiness, stability and clear thinking. They have given me the opportunity to make amends and change my behavior. I can make an apology when I can and should. I can ask for help. I can say that I understand how tough it must have been to be around me when I was flying high or secluded in my black hole or grabbing alcohol, drugs, exercise, work, shopping, whatever, to end the pain.

I will accept, without whacking myself over the head with guilt, that some people are still angry. My apology and my explanation would cause them more pain. For these people, I will accept that the best I can do is apologize to them in my heart, pray for their happiness and do my best to never behave that way again.

Finally, I will forgive myself and never forget that I am responsible - not others - for my happiness and mental health.

These are the lessons of those little pills.

Stigma, stigma everywhere

If you don't think there is a stigma about depression and mental illness, read on.

A woman goes to the doctor and is diagnosed with depression. Her doctor wants to prescribe an antidepressant. She agrees to take it. But the doctor is concerned that word will get out that she's on antidepressants. The doctor wants to use her maiden name on the prescription.

She tells the doctor she is not ashamed of having depression and that it is not necessary to use her maiden name. The doctor disregards her request and calls in the prescription using her maiden name. The woman goes to the pharmacy and is thoroughly embarrassed when the pharmacist can't find her prescription. Then she remembers the doctor's suggestion. The pharmacist finds her prescription under her maiden name.

Another woman has suffered with depression since she was a teen. Now she has a job with medical benefits. She is young and wants to move up in the company, or maybe take an even better job with another company. But she is afraid that a diagnosis of a mental illness on her record will mark her. And so she decides to pay for her medicine out of her pocket. Therapy, which she knows she needs, is just too expensive.

I know a therapist who told me she once stayed up most of the night to prepare for a hearing before a team of insurance company doctors. The insurance company had refused her patient's claim because the therapist is out of the network. So the therapist went before the panel to try to convince them that her patient needs specialized therapy, in which she is trained. None of the network therapists have the training. The panel said they would give her an answer that day. A month has passed. She still hasn't heard.

Good luck trying to get disability insurance if you have a mental illness and are self-employed.

You think that drug test at work just detects illegal drugs like marijuana, cocaine and heroin? Think again. Many comprehensive drug-screening programs include a TCA panel, which detects a class of antidepressants called tricyclics.

Shall I go on? The stigma is everywhere.

If you have depression, this isn't news. You already know this and more. You know that your co-workers will make wisecracks behind your back about whether you stopped taking your meds if you act a little too hyper or a little too blue.

You know better than to say you need a day off work because you can't concentrate or sit still. So, you lie. And God help you if you leave your prescription in the medicine cabinet or on the kitchen counter when you have a promising date.

I never knew these things until I was diagnosed with depression. Probably because I thought I didn't know anyone with depression.

Turned out, I was wrong.

Mindfulness

One of my girlfriends leaned over and whispered in my ear the other day. "From one depressed girl to another, you're going downhill. You know that, right?"

Well, I knew something was going on. I hadn't been feeling right for a few weeks. My memory was kind of off and the glass was starting to look half empty. I wasn't despondent. I still had really great days. But I felt it seeping back in.

The dead give away? My wrinkles weren't quite as deep. The upside of depression is that we let all of our facial muscles relax. Botox without the botulism.

I was in denial. I hadn't wanted to say anything to my therapist. I figured she already knew. My daughter was on it. "What's wrong, Mom?" she kept asking.

I tried to convince myself that it was just hormones, just the anniversary of my mother's death, just running into my ex and his new girlfriend, whom he has already moved in with, thank you very much. It's just life, I told myself, even though I wasn't believing it.

I went about 12 hours one day before I remembered that all I had eaten was a banana and a granola bar.

This is depression. And I don't want to be sick again. The odds are against me. A 1997 study found that depression "is a chronic, lifelong illness, the risk for repeated episodes exceeds 80 percent, patients will experience an average of four lifetime depressive episodes of 20 weeks duration each."

The good news: Researchers are all over this. They have found that "once a person has recovered from an episode of depression, a relatively small amount of negative mood can trigger a large amount of negative thoughts," according to the University of Oxford Center for Suicide Research. "When this happens, the old habits of negative thinking will start up again . . . and a full-blown episode of depression may be the result."

Their research has shown that "Mindfulness-Based Cognitive Therapy" significantly reduced the risk of relapse for those with at least three prior episodes of major depression. Simple breathing, yoga stretches, therapy, education and listening to tapes helped participants see the patterns of their thinking and to recognize when their mood begins to slip.

"The discovery that, even when people feel well, the link between negative moods and negative thoughts remains ready to be reactivated, is of enormous importance," according to the Oxford Web site. "It means that sustaining recovery from depression depends on learning how to keep mild states of depression from spiraling out of control."

Ah. This I can understand. This I can do. This makes sense. Mindfulness.

The trinity of treatment

I went to a fund-raiser luncheon last week. Some of the world's top researchers on depression spoke passionately about their efforts to help us. I heard about women and depression, children and depression and substance abuse and depression.

It was all very impressive until the physician researching substance abuse and depression made his presentation. He spoke about the frequency of these two mental illnesses occurring together, called co-morbidity, and the terrible toll it takes on addicts and alcoholics and their families.

He spoke about medicines being developed to treat alcoholism. His research showed that children with ADHD who are not treated with medications are twice as likely to become substance abusers. Not once in his presentation did he mention 12-step programs, the most successful treatment for substance abuse, ever.

And therein, in my opinion, lies the problem with mental health care in the United States. It's all about the drugs. Doctors often fail to understand that mental illness is a three-fold disease: mental, physical and spiritual. You can't just treat one. You must treat all three.

Some doctors don't like this. Psychotherapy, family sculpting, cognitive behavioral therapy, well, they're just not - how shall we say it - serious. They're not real medicine. They're too new age-y. And don't even think about mentioning "a higher power."

We all need to stop believing that balancing the chemicals in our brains is going to cure our illness. A pill is not always the answer. The reason? Because in living with our depression, we often pick up some nasty character defects which, if not treated, can trigger another depression. I'm talking about things like codependency, anger control and low self-esteem.

We dread our feelings. We either avoid them because we fear they will launch us into another depression or indulge in them because we don't know how to stop. You're either a shark and you just keep moving to get away from your feelings or you're like one of those statues of the Virgin Mary that mysteriously cries and cries without explanation.

We're messed up. We need the help of a "higher power." It could be God. But it doesn't have to be. A higher power is just an acceptance that it's going to take a power greater than yourself to handle this disease.

Your higher power can be your friends, your therapist, your dog, your partner or your mother-in-law. Or not.

It's humbling to ask for - and accept - help. But our minds, our bodies and our spirits depend on it.

My brain is back

I have almost finished reading a novel. It is the first novel I have read since I slipped into a deep depression nearly 10 months ago. Ten months - enough time to have a baby. A very long time for someone who loves to read and write.

It is a good book. On Saturday night, I will host my book club and I will finally be able to participate again in a discussion about our book. It is a simple thing but when something this precious is suddenly taken from you and then returned it is pure joy.

I had no idea that depression affected a person's memory and concentration. I thought depression was just immense, immobilizing sorrow. When I picked up the newspaper that for 20 years I have written for, I was stunned and disoriented by my inability to focus. I read the same paragraph over and over and asked myself, what did that say? It was as if my car had been stolen and I was standing in the parking lot turning around, looking, looking, looking in disbelief. I was so scared. What if it never comes back? I asked those treating me: "What if I can never write again? What if I'm never able to concentrate long enough to read the newspaper? What will I do? Who will I be? How will I support my daughter?

My therapist and psychiatric nurse practitioner assured me my memory and concentration would return. It would take time. But it would return. "You're sure, right?" I asked over and over.

It did, slowly, and it turns out that's perfectly normal. A Finnish study of 174 people suffering major depression showed that after six months of medication and therapy, those who felt better reported fewer memory problems and improved their scores on memory tests.

Once again it's all about that chemical imbalance in our brains. Brain imaging has shown that brain cell activity in the frontal lobes, behind the forehead, is reduced when we have depression. People with depression have lower levels of serotonin, a chemical that regulates blood flow and our ability to feel pleasure. The lower serotonin level may explain the reduced brain activity, according to the Newsletter of the Memory Disorders Project at Rutgers University.

Our brains also skew the types of memories that bubble up: "A depressed person tends to recall mostly the negative, unhappy experiences," according to the newsletter's Web site. "This can appear to family and friends as a loss of memory. It also reinforces the person's drab and negative view of life, fueling the depression."

I'm happy to say that my brain is back. Actually, it seems to be much better. I can now remember phone numbers without writing them down. Everything seems to be intact and I have a new respect for my noggin. I even do little mental exercises, like writing with my left hand to see what comes out of the other side of my brain.

But mostly, I just read. Newspapers, the trashy tabloids at the checkout, and my beloved book club books. I even got new bifocals. I am back on the couch, Sunday afternoon, with my dog snuggled between my feet, my glasses on my nose and a book in my hands. I am happy and I never want to forget it.

Managing depression on the job

Here's something to think about if you are a boss.

Say you hear about an illness that is the costliest disability among workers. When this disease strikes, workers are out for weeks, sometimes months. Before they become disabled their productivity tanks and their attitude is rotten. They're often late and sometimes don't bother to come into the office at all. They don't dress as well as they used to and sometimes you can smell last night's nightcap on their breath. They drag down the other employees.

Wouldn't you want to learn something about this disease? Wouldn't you want to find out if there is a way to prevent or detect it? Wouldn't you want to know how to keep these workers healthy? We're not just talking about the well-being of your work force - we're talking about money.

This disease is real. It is depression. In America, depression costs employers an estimated $79 billion in lost productivity and absenteeism alone.

The Global Burden of Disease Study conducted by the World Health Organization, the World Bank and Harvard University found that "major depression ranked second only to ischemic heart disease in magnitude of disease burden in established market economies."

Major depression "is the leading cause of disability worldwide among persons age 5 and older," the study concluded. All mental illnesses account for over 15 percent of the burden of disease worldwide, more than the burden of all cancers.

When your managers and supervisors are attending those training seminars sponsored by the human resource department, why aren't they learning about these diseases? There is training on carpal tunnel syndrome and ergonomic chairs and how to properly lift heavy objects - ailments that generate workers compensation claims. What training is there on how to handle a depressed or alcoholic employee? Almost none. Instead, they are taught to "recommend the EAP (employee assistance program)."

Employers need to understand that supervising a mentally ill worker is not like supervising a worker with diabetes or asthma or sciatica or migraines. You can't just send the worker home. In fact, sending home an alcoholic with depression or allowing him to work at home might be the worst thing you can do. Requiring a bipolar employee to oversee a new project might be too much. Would you ask an employee recovering from back surgery to sit for a daylong training seminar?

When a worker with depression returns to the job, do you take as much interest in his illness and recovery as you would a worker with recovering from pneumonia? Does your body language and the tone of your voice say that you don't believe depression and alcoholism are real diseases?

I am blessed with an amazingly understanding boss, who doesn't hesitate to reel me in when she sees me going down. To her, it's not about the bottom line, it's about me. So, remember, when you deal with a mentally ill worker, compassion, understanding and open-mindedness can reap huge, expected profits.

Try, try, try again

Suppose you have this really bad earache. You go to the doctor, and she gives you a prescription, and after a few days, your earache is actually worse. What would you do?

You would call the doctor and tell her the medicine isn't working, right?

Now, say you have depression, and you feel really bad. You go to the doctor, and she gives you a prescription, and after a few days, maybe weeks, your depression is worse. What would you do?

A lot of us would not call the doctor and tell her the medicine isn't working. We would stop taking it and limp along with our depression, hoping the black drape would eventually lift, while complaining that antidepressants don't work.

The initial results of the nation's largest clinical trial for depression found that only one-third of the participants reached remission with the first antidepressant prescribed. That means about 67 percent of us aren't going to feel better with the first antidepressant we try.

But the good news from the study is that 33 percent of those who did not respond to the first antidepressant they tried did achieve remission when they tried another antidepressant or added another to their regimen. And another 20 percent responded when a third drug was tried or added.

Now, in a perfect world, doctors would know this. And they would also know about a recommendation by the American Psychiatric Association that says, "In practice, the frequency of monitoring during the acute phase of a pharmacology (drug therapy) can vary from once a week in routine cases to multiple times per week in more complex cases." Your doctor would schedule you for weekly checkups to see how you are doing.

But that probably isn't going to happen. Another study found that 83 percent of adults did not see a clinician for a follow-up in the first month of antidepressant therapy.

Where does that leave you? It leaves you alone at the bottom of your black hole unless you become your own advocate. Believe me, I know you're not feeling like Norma Rae right now. Still, you have to speak up. You have to push and question and demand these follow-up visits.

There is no one-size-fits-all antidepressant. It's not like a Z-PAK - you take one little antibiotic pill for five days, and the infection is gone. It's more like trying to keep the pH balanced in a swimming pool. It takes constant monitoring and tweaking to keep that water clear.

Once again, it comes down to you. It's not right. It's not fair. But you're going to have to demand your way back to happiness.

Treating men and depression

I got a call last week from a good friend. I knew before she said a word it was bad news. A friend had killed himself.

This is the third man I have known who killed himself in the past year.

He had had a nasty divorce, like the others. He had children, like the others. He had people who loved him, like the others. He had depression, like the others.

I can't tell you exactly how I feel. I am shocked. I am sad. I am angry. I am speechless. I have a feeling in my chest that I didn't wake up with this morning. I know other things contributed to these men's decision to kill themselves. Still, I can't help thinking how insidious depression is. If only it manifested itself like other diseases that easily convince us things are getting worse, like a growing tumor on a CAT scan or a trembling hand with Parkinson's.

Depression is just there, disguising itself as sadness, as anger or indifference. On the outside we look normal, maybe a little thinner or heavier or angrier or quieter. People around us see our behavior but they can't see the horrible chemical imbalance in our brain. We're just behaving differently, too self-absorbed, feeling sorry for ourselves, drinking too much, sleeping too much.

If you are a man and you have thought about killing yourself, know this: Women make more suicide attempts than depressed men, but depressed men are far more successful. Four times as many men die by suicide than women, according to the National Institute of Mental Health.

"In light of research indicating that suicide is often associated with depression, the alarming suicide rate among men may reflect the fact that men are less likely to seek treatment for depression," according to the NIMH. "Many men with depression do not obtain adequate diagnosis and treatment, which may be lifesaving."

It's estimated that between 7,000 and 12,000 children lose a parent to suicide every year. I have stood beside a casket and watched a child look at the father who decided his pain was too much to endure. "Did ya touch him?" the boy asked me. "He's so cold." I never want to see or hear this again. I don't want to think about little boys with just a photograph of their father.

But I'm asking too much. There will be a service for my friend later this week. He has twin boys. They are 3 years old.

Gray days of winter

My flight landed in Detroit about noon on Dec. 26. Waiting in the aisle to get off the plane, I glanced out the window and it instantly hit me. I hadn't expected it. I had forgotten about it.

The sky was gray.

It was not the gray sky that I've grown accustomed to, living 22 years in Florida. Our gray skies here are filled with dramatic thunderheads, shades of gray and blue and sometimes an eerie green. The clouds swirl and explode and burst with thunder and lightning.

But the Michigan sky is flat and gray. There are no clouds, just one flat blanket that never changes, never moves or reveals its shape. It stalks me.

I realized that all those years living in the Midwest, I had suffered from seasonal affective disorder or SAD (how appropriate is that?). That miserable, despondent feeling didn't have a name back then. Thank God it does now and it is recognized as a significant trigger for depression.

March was my worst month. By then I was starved for sunlight. During the five months of winter, days with just of eight hours of light filtered through the oppressive gray cloud cover, I would slowly walk down a dark staircase into my black hole.

By March I had usually reached the bottom. I was depressed. On the first sunny days of April, with patches of dirty snow on the ground, I would put on my bathing suit, slather my body with baby oil and iodine and lie in the sun. It didn't matter that it was only 50 degrees.

The Mental Health Research Association estimates that as many as six of every 100 people in the United States might experience this winter depression. SAD is more common in women, and light therapy has proven effective in up to 85 percent of the diagnosed cases, the group found.

A study by the National Institute of Mental Health released in May found that "most patients will respond best to a low dose of the light-sensitive hormone melatonin in the afternoon in addition to bright light in the morning."

So, there you have it. Maybe try one of those SAD lamps or, ask your doctor about melatonin.

Or, better yet, move to Florida.

Self-medicating

Those of us who have depression tend to take things to the extreme.

We sleep too much. We eat too much or not enough. We spend too much. We drink too much. We smoke too much. We exercise too much. We'll do just about anything we believe will make us feel better and we'll do it too much because we feel so bad.

This is called self-medicating. For me, there is a strong correlation between how rotten I feel and how intensely I self-medicate. I have tried drugs, alcohol, exercise, working and cleaning. In the end, they all stopped working.

Looking back, I can see my first bouts of depression began when I was a kid. My mother would often tell me she knew how miserable I was and that college would be better. It wasn't.

Endorphins were my first drug. I discovered them at age 8. I was a top age-group swimmer. I swam butterfly, fast and hard. I liked the rush. But by age 14, I was sick of swimming. I tried my first drink. Then drugs. My new medicines.

For 25 years, they kind of worked. At least I thought so. But the hangovers were endless and left me deeper in despair. To avoid the despair, I worked like a machine and put Martha Stewart to shame, cleaning and straightening and exercising. If my newspaper reporting was good, if my house looked good, if I looked good, maybe I would feel good. I didn't.

I quit drugs and alcohol. That seemed to work for a few years. Then I felt rotten again. I tried to take it a little easier. That didn't work.

Then exercise stopped working. I went to a spin class at my gym at 6 a.m. I pedaled so hard that my lips flapped like a racehorse. Foam formed in the corners of my mouth. I got off the bike, and my legs quivered. There was no rush. Just despair.

That day, I closed my private pharmacy and asked for help. I got it. My therapist restricted my exercise and made me write down everything I ate to avoid more weight loss. My nurse practitioner prescribed real medication and explained why self-medicating didn't work. I stopped eating foods made with flour and drastically reduced my sugar intake. I cut back on caffeine. I meditated. I prayed. I began sleeping eight hours. I began to feel better.

So, at the end of your next pre-dawn 15-mile run, or 12-hour workday, or midnight vacuuming marathon, or third bottle of cabernet, ask yourself: Does this really make me feel better?

If not, ask for help.

Depression and your bundle of joy

I did not have postpartum depression.

I cannot even imagine what that must be like.

They say we forget the pain of childbirth when we see our child. But what if you went through all that pain, and then went into a black hole?

The sight of your bundle of joy leaves you despondent. The sound of your newborn's cries is a visceral reminder that you are miserable at the one time in your life when you should be ecstatic.

And everyone who loves you is on hand to remind you that you should be happy. "This should be the happiest time of your life." "Just look at that beautiful little baby. She looks just like you." "How can you not be happy?"

They look at you funny. They wonder - and you do, too - if you will be a good mother. You don't want to breastfeed. You don't want to change diapers. You don't want your stomach to look like a balloon that somebody deflated.

I had a hard enough time taking care of myself when I was in my black hole. I cannot understand how a mother with postpartum depression could care for an infant and herself.

God bless them.

Especially when some jerk like Tom Cruise has the nerve to say, "there is no such thing as a chemical imbalance." I don't care how many movies this guy has been in, how much money he has or who he married.

He's just a guy with a high school diploma who claims to know "the history of psychiatry." And somehow he believes he knows more about postpartum depression than Brooke Shields, who has not only given birth but also lived through a horrible bout of postpartum depression.

Here's what Shields had to say about postpartum depression. It sounds like she knows what she is talking about.

"Postpartum depression is caused by the hormonal shifts that occur after childbirth. During pregnancy, a woman's level of estrogen and progesterone greatly increases; then, in the first 24 hours after childbirth, the amount of these hormones rapidly drops to normal, nonpregnant levels. This change in hormone levels can lead to reactions that range from restlessness and irritability to feelings of sadness and hopelessness."

And here's what she did.

"I couldn't believe it when my doctor told me that I was suffering from postpartum depression and gave me a prescription for the antidepressant Paxil. I wasn't thrilled to be taking drugs. In fact, I prematurely stopped taking them and had a relapse that almost led me to drive my car into a wall with Rowan in the backseat. But the drugs, along with weekly therapy sessions, are what saved me - and my family."

What I like most about Shields' response published in The New York Times is this: "We are living in an era of so-called family values, yet because almost all of the postnatal focus is on the baby, mothers are overlooked and left behind to endure what can be very dark times. . . . Once we admit that postpartum is a serious medical condition, then the treatment becomes more available and socially acceptable."

Let's stop overlooking the mother after birth and judging her when she is depressed. Let's make sure she receives that same thorough care as her baby. And let's be grateful for brave women like Shields who can deliver a dignified and intelligent response to such an ignorant and arrogant diatribe.

And she did it without jumping on a couch.

Holding the hand that holds me down

In many ways, I have been holding the hand that holds me down.

I do things that make me sicker and more depressed without even realizing it. My behavior and character defects fuel the chemical imbalance in my brain. So the medicine is not enough.

I need someone to tell me, explain to me, what I am doing wrong.

Because I just don't see it.

At least today I recognize that I have a problem. They say that's the first step to getting better - realizing that there's something wrong. With me, my problem is called codependency. Yep. Another one of those psychobabble, boo-hoo, pseudo diagnoses that you hear about on afternoon talk shows.

Except it's real. It's not in the DSM manual thingy that all the insurance companies and clinicians use to determine if your ailment is covered. Still, it's real. If you are codependent, you will understand. If you aren't, it won't make much sense.

Codependency means there is no boundary between you and me. Your problems are my problems. I will do anything to try to solve them. If you ask me for a favor, I will automatically say "yes" even though there's a voice screaming "NO!" in my head. I can't set boundaries. I'd rather have my feelings hurt than yours. I will do whatever you ask. I want to make you happy. If you are happy, then I am happy. If you're mad, then I'm mad.

The running joke among us "codeps," as we call ourselves, is that we wake up, roll over and ask our partner how we feel today. Funny, huh?

We make great employees, friends and lovers. For a while. Until we get resentful because you don't want us to solve your problems and you don't want to be around a martyr and you don't like being smothered. Then our self-esteem tanks because you reject us. You are our emotional compass. Without you, we are lost. We have no idea who we really are because we're always molding ourselves to fit the people we think we love.

Then we get depressed.

This terminal caregiving is often seen in women. Especially women who grew up in alcoholic households where one parent smoothed over all the ugliness. That would be me. Because that's what I saw as a child, I thought it was normal.

The medicine for codependency is therapy. That is why the American Psychiatric Association recommends some kind of therapy in conjunction with medication for those of us with a major depressive disorder. The APA also recommends that the clinician work closely with the therapist. How often does that happen?

I got lucky. I gave my therapist and nurse practitioner permission to talk about me and they did. I took my meds and took my therapist's advice: go to a treatment center that specializes in codependency. I did. A whole week in the middle of nowhere learning to say "no" as a complete sentence. Best week of my life.

I still don't like saying "no." It makes me uncomfortable. When I do, I feel like I have to explain myself and apologize. Except when I say "no" to my dog. Then there are no explanations or apologies.

And she still loves me.

I just hope everyone else will.

Me? Angry?

When I finally began crawling out of my black hole and could concentrate long enough to read, someone suggested a book called *Women, Anger and Depression.*

Anger?

Moi? Surely you jest. I'm not angry, maybe just a little mad.

Boy, was I wrong. I wasn't just angry. I had rage. Kind of like that monster that rips through Sigourney Weaver's shipmate's chest in *Alien.*

You'd never know it because when I was a little girl I was told things like "good girls don't . . ." and "nice girls should . . ." and "keep your voice down." I believed it. So did a lot of women. Every time we got mad, someone was there to remind me that good girls just don't do that.

Good girls played with dolls. We did sports where we didn't touch each other. We didn't get to put on a helmet and bash into each other or wrestle around on a mat. We didn't slap each other upside the head, give wedgies, snap towels or put each other in a headlock.

As we got older, we got jobs that required decorum. We didn't get to take the claw end of a hammer and demolish a wall or pick up a jackhammer and pulverize a piece of concrete. Even now we get funny looks when we yell at the ref at our kids' soccer games. Or when we whistle between our teeth. Or when we cuss at a missed putt on the golf course.

Sure, I can hold my own in a heated verbal joust. But I walk away with a knot in my gut and my hands shaking. I must have done something wrong, I think. Now they're gonna think I'm a bitch. No one taught me how to "do" anger. The closest we came to anger in my childhood home was raging silence.

When that little girl grew up and something happened that should have made her angry, she would say, "I'm just sad," or "It's just not worth getting worked up about," or "He's probably just having a bad day," or "He didn't really mean to do that."

I just stuffed it. Denied it. I had decades worth of fermented anger.

Depression, I learned, is anger turned inward. I had enough anger inside to fuel a severe clinical depression. To get better and stay healthy

I was told to take my medications, continue my therapy and get rid of that anger.

OK. How?

My therapist whipped out a whiffle bat. I cringed. "A whiffle bat?"

"It makes a lot of noise when you hit the chair with it," she said.

I liked the bat idea but the whiffle seemed wimpy. Once I realized how much anger I had, I needed a real bat and real noise - like glass breaking. I found a metal bat, a junkyard and a green pickup truck that now has no windows, headlights, grill or front driver's side quarter-panel.

I don't recommend this kind of anger therapy. My hands were blistered and every muscle between my neck and small toe was sore for a week. My therapist was not pleased. However, it did work. And I can assure you that there are few experiences in a woman's life more satisfying than busting a truck window with a metal bat.

Today, I'm learning to be a woman of dignity, grace and anger. It is not easy. I am not good at it. But if it will keep me from falling back into my black hole, I'll do it.

Just not with a bat.

Holiday gratitude

Is it me, or is just about every holiday classic about depression?

At first I thought it was just George Bailey, the financially strapped father of a passel of noisy kids in *It's a Wonderful Life*. Then there's Scrooge and The Grinch. And what's the deal with that mother in *Miracle on 34th Street*? Shall I go on?

How about The Littlest Angel who dies, goes to heaven and can't keep his halo on straight, can't sing on key with the seraphim and misses his dog? Or that country-western song about that little boy who wants to buy his dying momma those shoes? Then there's Elvis and *Blue Christmas*. Or the upbeat *Do They Know It's Christmas?* about people starving in Africa.

If you are in a depression during the holiday season you've got your own little holiday drama going on. But we can take a cue from these folks. We can look beyond the magic of Santa or an angel and find what lifted them out of their black holes.

No, not Lexapro or Wellbutrin, although that probably would have helped.

It was gratitude.

The hardest thing to find when you're in your black hole is gratitude. Hopelessness, loneliness, remorse, self-pity and worthlessness are right down there with you, gripping your hands. But if you can find just one little speck of gratitude down there, just one little crumb, you're on your way up and out.

George Bailey's gratitude came from seeing what the world would be like had he not been born. Scrooge's gratitude came in a dream, when he saw how his selfishness infected anyone who crossed his path and that he still had a chance to change. And so on.

For me, gratitude came with a beautiful teenage daughter, patient and caring friends, four paws and a wet nose, and disability insurance.

So, ask yourself today, can I find one thing, one little thing this holiday season to be grateful for? Can I hang onto that gratitude right now? Can I use this one tiny morsel of gratitude to let faith and hope into my miserable life? Am I willing to do this?

I wish I could tell you there's an angel who's going to lift you out of your black hole. I wish Santa could take away your pain with a present under a beautiful tree. But that's not going to happen. This isn't the movies. It's your life. Find that one thing, and hold onto the thought of it.

And if you can find nothing to be grateful for this Christmas Eve, know this: It's a privilege to talk to you each week. And for that - for you - I am grateful.

All I want for Christmas

If you think shopping for the mother-in-law is tough, try holiday shopping for a friend in a major clinical depression.

Now there's a challenge. You could buy this friend a winning Lotto ticket and it would mean about as much as, well, a piece of paper with numbers on it. Seriously, we lose interest in stuff when we're in a depression. This is a bonus for you holiday shoppers trying to save a buck. We're like a cheap date.

Let me begin with what not to buy someone in a depression. Do not give us books on depression. For starters, our attention span is so short and our thinking so jumbled that we can't read more than a few sentences. And we really don't want to read about how depressed someone else is anyway.

Next, don't buy us funny movies. I tried watching *Something About Mary* when I was depressed and it only made me more depressed when I couldn't laugh at Ben Stiller's zipper crisis. Don't give us anything that will remind us that *It's The Most Wonderful Time of the Year*. That means no Christmas ornaments or dreidels, no Elvis singing *Blue Christmas*.

Music actually hurt my ears when I was at my lowest.

Also, be careful on the food front. First, take a good look at us. Have we lost weight? Have we gained weight? If we've lost weight, food could be a good thing. But remember, fudge, pies and cookies all have lots of sugar. If we're not eating much to start with and we inhale a bunch of sugar, it's going to seriously mess with moods, kind of like it does with your annoying little nieces and nephews. If we've gained weight, and we're feeling especially rotten about our body image, giving us fudge is like putting a crack pipe in front of crackhead.

Ix-nay on the vacuum cleaner - even if it's a Dyson. Double ix-nay on sexy lingerie, as the last thing we want to do is what's involved after it's removed. Don't even think about a bottle of wine (a depressant). Or a puppy, goldfish, kitten or anything that needs to be fed or could poo on the floor.

What's left? How about this: If your friend has a pet, take the dog to the dog park or clean the litter box; if they have a car, wash it; if they wear clothes, wash them; if they don't have groceries, go to the grocery store and buy some - especially something healthy. Offer to clean the house or, if you have the dough, hire a cleaning service. Deliver dinner for a week and offer to keep them company during a meal.

Take us out for coffee - not to a hip Starbucks with funky music and funkier "baristas" - whatever the heck they are. Try a quiet little restaurant or a Dunkin' Donuts. Someplace where we don't have to worry about what we look like. Watch out for manicures or pedicures or hair appointments. We already know we look like hell and it's excruciating to go to a salon where everyone looks mah-velous. A massage would be wonderful, especially at home.

The best gift? Just be there. You don't have to say anything. In fact, it might be better if you don't say anything. Just listen and sympathize. Don't judge. Don't tell us how much we have to be grateful for this holiday season. Call us and even if we don't answer, leave a nice message. Don't let us be alone on Christmas Eve, New Year's Eve or during Hanukkah. Smile at us.

Let us know that we are a gift in your life.

The angels on my suicide list

I watched the holiday classic *It's a Wonderful Life* the other night.

It seemed to me - after having gone through a major clinical depression myself this year - that this is a movie about a guy who is suffering through a major depressive episode.

George Bailey is so depressed, that he tries to kill himself by jumping off a bridge on Christmas Eve. Besides being faced with a catastrophic financial loss, Christmas is bearing down on him - the wife, the kids and the big Christmas tree in the living room that he's expected to help decorate.

He freaks out, snaps at the wife and kids, abandons the family and goes to the local bar to toss back a few and contemplate suicide. Sound familiar?

That's where reality ends. An elderly, good-natured but bumbling angel named Clarence jumps in the icy water to save George and gives him a chance to see what life would be like if he hadn't been born.

This got me thinking. What if I had an angel like Clarence? But instead of showing me what the world would be like if I had not been born, he would show me what the world would be like if I had killed myself. I know that's a little morose but it got me thinking of all the people who really would miss me.

Of course, there is my daughter, probably even my ex-husband, my brother and sister and all my nieces and nephews. My friends - and today I have a lot of friends - my hairdresser, the guys at the gym who see me at my roll-out-of-bed best, the women in my book club, everyone who comes to my Christmas Eve open house, my co-workers (some of them, anyway) the folks at the mental health center where I volunteer, and, obviously my dog.

Really, I do have a lot of people in my life who would be devastated. I need to remember this the next time I slide into my black hole. I need to find some way to think about these people when I'm down there and I think I'm all alone and that it will never get better.

I decided to make a list of everyone who really would be upset by my suicide. Within 10 minutes I had over 100 names. I quit when a few seconds separated each name that popped into my head, like a bag of popcorn ready to take out of the microwave. That seemed like enough. I proved my point.

I will keep the list. I could not have made it when I was in my hole. Because when I'm down there, I convince myself that everyone - including the dog - would be better off without me. I'm going to put it in the top drawer of my bedside table. I will add to it. It's my gratitude list. I will promise to pull it out the next time I am in my black hole and my mind wanders to hoses and car exhaust.

I really don't need a Clarence. You see, I already have more than 100 Clarences.

Merry Christmas and Happy Hanukkah to all of you.

Suicide: It starts like this

There is nothing quite like waking up when you never expected to wake up again.

You stare at the ceiling and a word that can't be printed here comes to mind. Your mind is capable of handling only that word - one syllable. After a few moments, you close your eyes again and think, "(one-syllable word), it didn't work."

"I'm not dead."

This is what it's like to fail at suicide. You think, "I've failed at everything else in my life - why not suicide, too?" If you're not in a hospital hooked up to a machine, you drag yourself to the bathroom and throw up. You're not dead but you're halfway there. Your body's will to live is stronger than your mind's will to die and you just let your body take over. Your brain just doesn't have the energy to fight the body right now. "Whatever," you think.

I've been there. I was just a teenager. A seriously depressed teenager. No one ever knew. I threw up and pretended I had the flu.

I can tell you this: You get a little better each time you try. That's why in April, when I started wondering if my hybrid car would produce enough toxic fumes to kill me, I knew I had to do something. To get help. At first I found the thought amusing in a twisted kind of way. That's usually how it starts.

It's just a little thought. You dismiss it quickly. But it keeps coming back. You indulge it a little more each time. You start wondering where you can get things - pills or a gun or a Web site that will tell you how to do it. You contemplate the diameter of your tail pipe and a garden hose. How would you hook them together? Duct tape?

You start wondering where - the beach, the back yard, a parking lot. Who would find you? You imagine your funeral . . .

You tell yourself these are just thoughts. You wouldn't do something like that. Come on. But they keep coming back and you can't seem to get rid of them. It starts making sense. You just want out. Out of everything. Life is horrible. You're such a failure. You don't fit in. You don't know what's wrong with you. Nothing is right. Just do it. End the anguish.

This is depression.

On my first visit to my psychiatric nurse practitioner she made me sign a legal document promising that I would call a suicide hotline if I was going to kill myself. What a joke, I thought. Like a piece of paper was going to stop me. But I did think about that stupid piece of paper and the nuns in third grade telling me that people who kill themselves go straight to hell.

And I thought about my daughter.

She is what they call an "anchor." She is my anchor to life. When I was in my black hole, I looked at my therapist square in the eye and said, "Anything happens to her, I'm outta here." I meant it.

Today, after faithfully taking my medications, weekly therapy and a lot of prayers, I realize I have lots of anchors. Friends, family, a home with leaky plumbing, my dang dog and my gorgeous daughter. They need me as much as I need them.

So if you know someone in a black hole, be their anchor. Let them know you need them.

Desperately.

Christine Stapleton

God as I understand him, her or it

I don't think you can go through a major clinical depression - or any life-threatening disease - without giving some thought to a higher power.

God. Allah. Yaweh. The Force. Whatever you believe in or don't believe in. Being utterly despondent will either confirm your belief in a Godless universe, reaffirm your faith in a loving God or convince you that someone up there has it in for you.

I can understand. I can't judge. All I know is something kept me going and it wasn't me.

I was raised a Catholic. I left the church. I came back to the church. I consider myself a pretty lame practicing Catholic. I never made it to Mass during my depression. But I prayed. On my knees, every morning and every night. They were foxhole prayers. I don't think God minded at all.

I know there is a God. I can't prove it. I won't even try. I just know. I know because he touched me twice - the first time I raised my newborn daughter to my breast to nurse her, and one winter day, sitting alone at our family's kitchen table, crying at my mother's imminent death and feeling something from behind - like the breeze that used to blow us across a frozen lake when we were kids - our jackets wide open to catch the wind, our skates crackling across the ice.

I just know.

Still, I have to admit I was not real happy with my God while I was in that black hole. Actually, I was pissed. She had abandoned me. He was testing me. She was punishing me. He was not being fair. I begged. I pleaded. I made promises. I cursed.

But I never lost contact.

You don't hear God mentioned much when people talk about treating depression. You hear about a lot of drugs. You hear about therapy and psychodrama and beating the heck out of pillows with whiffle bats. The God issue is an inside job, something each of us resolves in our own way. Privately.

Consider this: When you're in your black hole, what have you got to lose by saying a little prayer? Even if there is no God, what do you lose? A few moments when you have asked a power greater than yourself for

106

help? Maybe just asking someone or something for help is the first step to getting better.

If God does exist, then maybe he'll listen and you'll become happy, joyous and free. Maybe you'll even have a wonderful dream that George Clooney can't keep his hands off you.

I don't know. I don't have all the answers.

What I know for sure, today, is that I am happy. And I thank my God.

Alcoholism and depression

It's one of those chicken-or-the-egg debates.

Can the disease of alcoholism cause the disease of depression? Or, can self-medicating for depression using drugs and/or alcohol create an alcoholic or addict?

If you're an alcoholic and/or an addict and you suffer from depression, it doesn't really matter. Let's leave that debate to the researchers. Either way, you've got a double whammy. You have two of the most socially unacceptable mental illnesses. So unacceptable, in fact, that many people don't even recognize them as diseases.

How many people do you know who believe alcoholism is just a character defect even though the American Medical Association recognized it as a disease nearly 50 years ago, subsequently joined by the American Psychiatric Association, the American Hospital Association, the American Public Health Association, the National Association of Social Workers, the World Health Organization and the American College of Physicians?

Probably plenty. They sound a lot like the people who can't understand why a week's vacation, a funny movie or a walk on the beach won't cure your depression. Being sick is bad enough. Having people judge you because of illnesses is worse. It only makes us sicker. And there are a lot of us being made sicker by these two diseases.

The National Mental Health Association estimates 37 percent of alcohol abusers and 53 percent of drug abusers also have at least one serious mental illness. Of all people diagnosed as mentally ill, 29 percent abuse either alcohol or drugs.

That's a lot of really sick people. So sick, they're even ostracized by their own.

Take the case of an alcoholic with depression. The depressed alcoholic gets involved in a recovery program only to learn that "mind altering" drugs are verboten and many recovering alcoholics consider antidepressants "mind altering" drugs. These recovering alcoholics - many with no more than a high school diploma - encourage the depressed alcoholic to stop taking their antidepressants. Or worse, they refuse to counsel and work with them.

Meanwhile, that same depressed alcoholic is afraid to talk to co-workers, friends and family about his depression because of the Tom Cruise syndrome.

So, the illnesses talk to each other. The depression tells the alcoholism that another drink will solve everything. The alcohol - itself a depressant - tells the depression, "Thanks for giving me a reason to drink."

If you think you haven't heard about people who have to deal with this dilemma, let me mention a few: Robin Williams, Ernest Hemingway, Drew Barrymore, Kurt Cobain, and Carrie Fisher. And maybe you, your girlfriend or the guy swinging a hammer on a job site.

Just think about it the next time you pour yourself a stiff one.

Dying for the macho mentality

This one is for the guys.

Researchers estimate that in any given year, twice as many women (about 12 million) are affected by depression as men.

Bull.

I cannot accept that this is a "girlie condition." I will not perpetuate the woe-is-me stereotype of the despondent "gal" with the back of her hand raised to her brow.

I'm sick. And so are a lot of guys. Here's what the National Institute of Mental Health has to say about it.

"We still do not know if depression is truly less common among men, or if men are just less likely than women to recognize, acknowledge and seek help for depression."

I believe that. A lot of the guys I know are unable to "recognize, acknowledge and seek help" for a lot of things. Like directions to a restaurant. Or turning on a computer. Or wrapping a birthday present.

It comes as no surprise that they won't ask for help when it comes to depression. The whole "pull yourself up by your bootstraps" kind of mentality means everything to them. Their manhood depends on it.

I feel sorry for men with depression. Not only do a lot of guys with depression not realize they are sick, even if they do, what can they do? Whom can they talk to about it? Not the guys at the Harley dealership. Not the guys on the job site. It's right up there with ED - erectile dysfunction.

So, let's take this opportunity to talk about men and depression.

"Research and clinical evidence reveal that while both women and men can develop the standard symptoms of depression, (men) often experience depression differently and may have different ways of coping with the symptoms," according to the NIMH.

Here it is in a nutshell:

"Instead of acknowledging their feelings, asking for help or seeking appropriate treatment, men may turn to alcohol or drugs when they are depressed, or become frustrated, discouraged, angry, irritable and sometimes violently abusive. Some men deal with depression by throwing themselves compulsively into their work, attempting to hide their depression from themselves, family and friends. Other men may respond to depression by engaging in reckless behavior, taking risks and putting themselves in harm's way."

Sound like a guy you know? Anger and irritability aren't just yelling and punching walls. It's sarcasm and those verbal right hooks we throw at those we love. Workaholism isn't just going to the office every now and then on Saturday morning. It's countless sleepless nights with proposals, projects and dollar signs racing through your head. Reckless behavior isn't just trying out your teen's skateboard. It can be an affair with a co-worker, visits to a massage parlor and too many hours on porn sites - always hoping that something or someone will blow away that dark cloud that's always hanging over your head.

Finally, a word about depression and sex. OK, some people experience adverse sexual side effects from taking antidepressants. Before you use that as an excuse not to get help, ask yourself this: What kind of sex life are you going to have if you're "frustrated, discouraged, angry, irritable and sometimes violently abusive"?

Sorry, not my kind of guy.

Monitor your meds

A good friend called me this morning. I didn't recognize her voice. She wasn't hysterical. She wasn't sobbing. She was through. Just through.

She was depressed. Her doctor had prescribed an antidepressant and told her to come back in a couple of months for a check-up.

My friend said she had been taking her antidepressant as prescribed. Now, she felt worse. She didn't have a plan to kill herself. But if she fell asleep and didn't wake up . . . oh well. Or if a car hit her while crossing the street . . . oh well.

"This is no way to live," she pleaded.

No, it isn't. Maybe it was the problems in her life. But maybe it was the antidepressant, some of which reportedly can make depression worse.

Maybe she wouldn't be in this condition if her doctor had followed the recommendations of the U.S. Food and Drug Administration and the American Psychiatric Association about prescribing antidepressants.

According to the FDA: "Adults being treated with antidepressant medications, particularly those being treated for depression, should be watched closely for worsening of depression and for increased suicidal thinking or behavior. Close watching may be especially important early in treatment, or when the dose is changed, either increased or decreased."

The American Psychiatric Association gets more specific: "In practice, the frequency of monitoring during the acute phase of pharmacotherapy (drug therapy) can vary from once a week in routine cases to multiple times per week in more complex cases."

What part of "week" is hard to understand? How many clinicians out there are writing prescriptions for antidepressants and telling their patients to come back in a month or two?

Apparently, a lot.

A study published in a peer-reviewed journal in August found that 66 percent of children and 83 percent of adults did not see a clinician for a mental health care visit in the first month of antidepressant therapy.

Even more troubling, 53 percent of children and 76 percent of adult patients still had no mental health care follow-up care during the first three months of taking antidepressants, according to the study.

OK, the study looked at patients given antidepressants between 2001-2003, just before the antidepressant scare became widespread. Still, it's disturbing.

I was lucky. When I finally got help for my depression I had the good fortune to be referred to a psychiatric nurse practitioner who not only quizzed me like a homicide detective but also required weekly visits for the first couple of months. She even called at home to make sure I was OK.

Thank God she did. Three weeks after beginning my antidepressant therapy I was worse. I became more despondent. "How long is this going to last?" I asked, slumped on her couch. Not long. She immediately changed my medication regime. Within a week I was starting to crawl out of my black hole.

My friend is still in hers.

Listen to your body – it's trying to tell you something

I left work early recently. I was tired.

Being "tired" has never seemed like a good enough reason to leave work. I felt guilty doing it. But these days, I listen to my body. I went home and slept for 12 hours.

I now see that, months ago, my body was trying to warn me before I slid into a deep clinical depression - my black hole - in April.

Five months earlier, my back went out. I was bending over the dishwasher and felt a twinge. I couldn't stand up. I had been going to the gym religiously, had done plenty of back and stomach exercises and stretching. I hadn't had a backache like that since I returned to the newsroom six weeks after having my daughter, also an incredibly stressful time.

About the same time my back went out, I noticed tightness in my chest. My heart pounded hard for no apparent reason, then quickly slowed down. I ignored it and plowed through the holidays, decorating the house and tree, sending out the holiday cards, hosting my annual Christmas Eve open house, shopping for and wrapping all the presents, baking Christmas cookies, cooking Christmas dinner and working full-time.

I finally called my doctor. He ordered a stress test and a CAT scan. My heart was fine.

But I was stressed. I had trouble sleeping. Had trouble eating. Had trouble concentrating and sitting still. I stared off into space. I hardly said a word to anyone. My 14-year-old daughter had a nervous look in her eyes. I told her she wasn't responsible for my happiness, that she had done nothing wrong. Still, I could feel her watching me.

Then my world imploded.

As an athlete, I had always considered myself in tune with my mind and body. I know, for instance, that I got an endorphin rush from exercising. I also knew how stress manifested itself: I got a tick in my eyelid during the 2000 election and a knot under my left shoulder blade during the 2004 hurricanes. Stress.

I realize now that for years, I have underestimated the connection between my mental and physical health. I didn't appreciate how well my mind and body work together - how well they try to take care of each other - despite my best efforts to ignore their messages.

You would think I'd have learned this lesson when my mother was diagnosed with colon cancer. Colon cancer? My mom? She ate well, didn't smoke, drank very little, exercised and consumed vast amounts of fiber. She was also depressed and worried incessantly. For decades. She died never knowing what caused her cancer

So, today, I'm going to listen to my body. I'm going to listen to my mind. I'm going to respect their relationship. I'm going to slow down when I am tired. I'm going to play when I need to have fun. I'm going to ask myself how I feel.

And I'm going to answer.

Is sadness safe?

I got sad a few weeks ago. It was the first time I had been sad since I lifted out of my black hole a month earlier.

It was my ex-boyfriend's birthday. A year earlier, I had thrown him a 50th birthday party. I thought of the fun I'd had designing the invitations, planning the food, being surrounded by good friends.

A year later, we weren't even speaking to each other. Sad. Sad. Sad.

Then it hit me: fear. Oh God, is this the start of another depression? Will I slide back into that hole? Is this how it starts?

Is it safe to be sad?

Feelings - I had learned from my treatment team - are not to be ignored. They are like the IRS. Deal with them now or the penalty will grow exponentially. You will be overwhelmed. No avoiding it.

I don't like feelings. When you suffer from depression, feelings are the enemy. I do anything to avoid them. I keep busy. So busy that I have no time to feel or even think about my feelings. I clean. I exercise. I read. I work. I do the laundry. I shop. I make dinner. Then I exercise some more. Clean some more. Read more. Work more. More. More. More.

God, just don't let me have to feel a feeling. Especially sad.

They told me I have to learn to do feelings. The medications will only correct the chemical imbalance in my brain. It is up to me to control my self-defeating behaviors.

Identify your feelings, they told me. Sit with your feelings, they said. Talk about your feelings. Write about your feelings. Express your feelings. They even gave me a long list of feelings.

Uh-huh. Right. OK. Can you say "psychobabble"? Enough with the feelings already.

If there is one thing I learned from childbirth, though, it's this: When you're in enough pain, you will do anything to end it. Push. Puff. Pant. Focus on a happy thought. Go ahead, stick a needle in my spine. Whatever. Bring on the wacky suggestions.

So I tried doing the feelings. I went with the sadness. I embraced it. I cried. I called my girlfriends. I wrote letters that I will never send. I cried some more. The sadness came in waves, and I didn't try to stop it. I let it roll over me.

I learned two things: 1. Cry enough, and your waterproof mascara will run. 2. The waves slowly become ripples. And, eventually, calm.

And I did not sink into my black hole. I had been sad. Just sad.

The sweet smell of relief

When things were bad, really bad, and I couldn't sleep, couldn't eat, couldn't watch TV, couldn't read, couldn't do anything but focus on my damn miserable self, my dog would save the day. Or night.

Bella, my 2 1/2 year old Weimaraner, would give me the look: "I need a walk. You need a walk. Let's walk - NOW."

So, I'd clip on her leash and let her drag me around the dark, quiet neighborhood. It was on one of those walks that I discovered the power of "huffing" or, as classier folks put it, "aromatherapy." Part of our walk would take us past a wooden fence that was covered in night-blooming jasmine.

I'd never paid much attention to night-blooming jasmine, probably because if I'm up in the middle of the night, when night jasmine blooms, it's because my daughter is sick, I have a flight to catch or I'm training for some kind of race. I'm not up to smell the roses, or jasmine.

But on those sad nights, the sweet exotic smell would hit me half a block away. When I got to the fence I would make Bella "sit" then "stay." Amazingly, she would. I shoved my nose into a cluster of the small white waxy flowers, closed my eyes and breathed in, slowly and deeply. For a split second, I felt fine. I stood at the fence for as long as Bella would tolerate it, then I'd continue walking, looking for another mailbox or fence covered with jasmine.

I was convinced that someone would call the cops and I'd be busted for huffing jasmine. I didn't care. Just a split second of feeling fine was worth it. I completely understood those odd addicts who get a rush off sniffing paint or glue. Thankfully, jasmine doesn't cause brain damage and isn't addicting. I planted some outside my bedroom.

Maybe there was something to this aromatherapy hoo-ha. Maybe my sense of smell could help me. I thought about my favorite smell - the fine, soft hair on my daughter's head when she was a baby. Unfortunately, my daughter is now 14 and won't let me sniff her head.

How about the Anthropologie store! That place smells pretty good. I went there and was shown a table of candles. I sniffed, found one I liked, then looked at the price tag. Who in their right mind pays $25 for a candle? Me. It was worth it.

I thought about my other senses. What about sound? I love music, but when I hit bottom I couldn't listen to anything. Even the television sounded tinny. As I got better, my love of music slowly returned. I pulled out my CDs and quickly discovered that this was not the time to listen to Sarah McLaughlin, Alanis Morissette, Nirvana or Rachmaninoff.

I needed music associated with better times. Some Beatles (sitting with my sister, screaming at the television during the Ed Sullivan show), a little Aerosmith (reminiscent of those teen make-out sessions in the basement) and a dash of the Grateful Dead (no comment).

My daughter began making CDs. Jack Johnson, G. Love, 311 and Sublime. But "our song" - she decided - was Lynyrd Skynyrd's *Free Bird*.

"Cuz I'm as free as a bird now, and that bird you cannot change. No that bird you cannot cha-a-a-a-a-nge."

I hope she's right.

The gift of those who "get it"

There are people who "get it" and people who don't "get it."

I used to be one of those people who thought they got it but really didn't have a clue.

I'm talking about depression.

I really didn't understand what it was. Even though I had been around people with depression and had read books on the topic, the best I could do was offer sympathy and support. Now, having been through a major clinical depression that left me unable to work for two months, I appreciate those people in my life who "get it." Actually, I get on my knees every night and thank God for those people.

We all form bonds with people who suffer from our ailments, whether it's the flu we share with our co-workers or the head lice our kids pick up at camp. We commiserate, we support each other, we feel connected. But depression robs us of the ability to carry on any meaningful conversation beyond our own misery. We aren't selfish. We are in so much anguish it is impossible for us to speak of anything else, if we can speak at all.

I look back and see that, when I was in my black hole, I needed my medications. I needed my therapy. I needed to make sure I had eaten. I needed to get out of bed. But what made me feel better when I was there, in that deep, dark hole, were my friends who "got it."

There was one who called every day with the same message: "I'm just calling to check in and see how you're doing today." This friend, a beautiful career woman always willing to lend a hand or a wisecrack, had suffered from depression since she was a teen, and had been in and out of hospitals. She shared her experiences with antidepressants like she was sharing recipes.

There was another friend, a reputable professional with an amazing home, brilliant husband and handsome sons, who took one look at me, shrugged her shoulders and said: "I need to be on hormones or antidepressants all the time. You should think about it." Somehow, that was all I needed: Permission to take the medicine I had resisted.

My other friend told me she suffers a major depression just about every year - not exactly what I wanted to hear. She looked me square in the eye and promised that even though I might endure another episode, I would know how to handle it, I would know that it wasn't going to last forever and I would know she would always be there for me. I know she is right. I know I can trust her. I know she "gets it."

And God bless a fourth friend, my guardian angel, diagnosed bipolar, who let me sit on her couch and weep, let me call her on the phone and weep, made sure I got out of the house. Most of all it was the look in her eyes. She didn't judge. She didn't tell me what to do. She didn't tell me to get a grip. She just nodded her head like a bobble doll and told me, "I get it."

I can't imagine how lonely it would be to go through a major depression without my friends. Even those of you who never suffered from this disease made it bearable. You taught me that it was OK to take off my superwoman cape and OK to let you help me. I couldn't have done this alone.

To my friends who have this disease, those of you who sacrificed your privacy and shared your experience, strength and hope - you saved my life.

To all of you, thank you.

My hypocrisy, my diagnosis

My therapist said the "B" word recently. Heaven help me.
Bipolar.
"I want the nurse to rule out bipolar," she said. Just like that.
The psychiatric nurse practitioner who monitors and prescribes my medications - a sort of benevolent grand inquisitor - officially declared

me clinically depressed in April after I sat on her couch, nearly catatonic, and answered a barrage of questions.

Depression is a label I can handle. Depression is almost trendy - even if it nearly kills you. But bipolar. Oooo, that's another ballgame. I don't want to be bipolar. Aren't people who are bipolar whacked? Doesn't the room vibrate when they walk in? Aren't they sooooo down that you want to tiptoe past them and hope they don't notice you?

Wow, is that me?

Apparently, it is. If I take a good look at myself, as others see me, I understand why my therapist would think that. At the end of a recent session I began talking about my job as a reporter at the newspaper - story ideas, stories I had written, stories I should have written, stories I want to write, stories I want other reporters to write, bad writing, good writing, bad reporting, good reporting - and I was off like a greyhound chasing Rusty around the track.

What shocks me is not the thought of being bipolar, it's my own bigotry about mental illness. In my mind, bipolar is socially less acceptable than depression. Schizophrenia is even worse than bipolar. Flat-out psychotic is, well, completely unacceptable. I have my own little caste system about mental illness!

And I'm the one who had always prided herself on being so compassionate and so understanding. "Oh, those poor, poor souls," I would think, secretly breathing a sigh of relief that at least I wasn't bipolar, or schizophrenic, or God-forbid, psychotic. What a hypocrite.

Still, I needed to know. At my next visit with the nurse practitioner, I stretched out the pleasantries for as long as possible. I told her how wonderful I was feeling. Finally, I casually slipped it into the conversation: "Oh, by the way, my therapist wants you to rule out bipolar. How was your weekend?"

My nurse practitioner hears and sees all. She gave me that look she gives before she starts with the questions. (She should have been a journalist.) "How's your sleep? How's your energy level? How's your appetite? Are your thoughts racing?" and on and on. There's no lying to her. You just gotta tell the truth.

I sat on her couch, feeling like I had just taken some kind of psychological pregnancy test and was waiting to see if the stick would turn blue. She described bipolar to me. Not me.

"I think you're hypo-manic," the nurse practitioner said. Hypomania is similar to mania but less severe. There are elevated moods, increased activity, decreased need for sleep, grandiosity, racing thoughts, unusual cheerfulness with a heightened state of creativity.

Hypomania can be treated with medication, she said. Phew.

But not my hypocrisy. There are no drugs for that.

Hating the illness, not the afflicted

I hate alcoholism. Everything about alcoholism I loathe. It is evil. It is toxic. It kills, robs and cheats. It has devastated my life.

I direct my anger and rage toward the illness and not the people afflicted with it. That is not to say alcoholism is an excuse for bad behavior. It is an explanation. Alcoholics, like myself, must make amends for our wrongs - whether we were under the influence or under the influence of the "isms" that turn us into human napalm bombs - scorching and maiming the lives of the innocent who just happened to be in our way.

Even ten years after my last drink this disease still afflicts me. I will never, ever be cured. And I must never, ever forget that. I still make choices in my sobriety that are wittingly and unwittingly driven by this disease. Sometimes I watch myself do it. Like watching myself hold my hand over a flame, knowing I will get burned but doing it anyway. "Why?" I ask myself. I knew the consequences but still I continue to put my hand over the flame.

After years of taking suggestions and working a program I have come to think of my disease as an alien hibernating in my body. For days and months it sleeps. I make healthy sober decisions. My depression and bipolar are in check and I avoid situations or relationships that will disturb my serenity, sobriety depression and bipolar. Then, like that little alien in Sigourney Weaver's chest in the movie *Alien*, that evil little guy unexpectedly awakens and rips through my chest, teeth-bared, writhing, thirsty and clawing at my other mental illnesses.

I am left stunned and wagging my head: "What the hell was that?" "Where did that come from?" It never ends. I must be constantly vigilant. I must test my motives, like a diabetic tests her blood.

It has taken years, and many raging swings of a foam bat against a pillow, to separate the disease from the nasty words, neglect and embarrassment caused by my own alcoholism and the alcoholics in my life. I think of my parents' cancer, and how easy it was to hate their cancer and not them. But I hated my father's alcoholism - and sometimes I hated him. I wish with all my might that I had been able to separate his alcoholism from him, the father who loved me immensely - the very best he could.

Today, as I wade through the wreckage of another alcoholic in my life, I will try to separate the disease from the person. Alcoholism is an explanation, not an excuse. I will carefully walk that line between allowing myself to be hurt and hurting the still sick, and suffering alcoholic. And I will pray that I can see that line today and stay on it.

Alone or lonely?

My therapist says I am "isolating." I tell her I am not. I just like to be alone. "No," she says. "You are isolating." "No," I say. "I just like to be alone."

We go back and forth like this for a while. Then she tells me that I have been isolating my whole life and reels off a few examples. Once again, she is right. When I was 7-years-old we moved from northern Wisconsin to Southwest Michigan. I went from being a pig-tailed tomboy in a small rural town to the new kid in a town with country clubs and summer cottages and family vacations to Vail. We belonged to the Elks Club, our summer vacations were to our relatives' farms and a veil was something girls had to wear on their head during Mass.

So, I took up competitive swimming. The perfect sport for a kid who doesn't fit in. You get to be with other kids but you don't have to talk - in fact, you can't talk. The fashion-playing field is leveled. Speedo made only a few bathing suits back in those days: A bathing suit was a bathing suit. I kicked butt, swimming butterfly for the blue ribbons as much as to pummel the country-club kids who made fun of our vending machines and "rustic" locker rooms at the Elks Club.

In seventh-grade I transferred from a middle-class Catholic school where we all wore the same uniforms, to a public junior high school where kids wore button-down collared shirts, corduroy Levis and sweaters tied around their necks. I took up solitary pastimes, like reading, writing, listening to my albums and playing the guitar. I tried to fit in but always felt left out - until I discovered alcohol, which made me the life of the party.

The first two years of college I finagled my own dorm room. I lived alone, but among a floor of other co-eds. I felt most comfortable in either a bar or the library - where I was not expected or encouraged to carry on a conversation. Even today, a library is my favorite public venue. It took decades to find a hair salon that didn't make me cringe. I am gifted at the art of small talk - just keep asking people questions about themselves. I can't stand personal phone calls. I like texting.

I like working in the yard, hanging clothes on the clothesline, riding my bike, walking my dog and the ultimate in solitary sports - scuba diving. I still love reading and writing. The iPod is one of the greatest inventions ever. Put those ear buds in and you can be in a crowed without hearing others or speaking.

I love being alone. What's wrong with that?

"You love it because it is familiar," my therapist told me. "But that does not mean it is good. It is an unhealthy behavior that you have practiced for so long that it feels natural and comfortable. It fuels your depression."

I am really trying to change. I have lots of friends who would love to be closer to me. For some reason, I won't let them. I don't call them, unless I need something. I don't have parties. I don't join neighbors for their monthly Happy Hour. I don't want to.

I see that I must change. I am trying. These are the behaviors that my alcoholism, bipolar and depression thrive on. Sometimes it is like they talk to me. "Hey, you could sit here and drink a bottle of wine and no one would know." "Brooding is so much better when you do it alone." "With all this energy why not paint the bathroom? What else have you got to do?"

I see it now as clearly as my therapist. I have got to change. I will.

If my mental illnesses could choose an occupation...

I am probably in the worst occupation for a middle-aged, bipolar woman with depression and alcoholism: reporter at a daily newspaper. I live with perpetual deadlines. I must be creative and productive under pressure. I am constantly bombarded with the sound of police scanners, telephones, reporters and editors hashing out stories. I don't write happy stories. The people I write about have either done something wrong, had something wrong done to them, were caught doing something wrong or witnessed something go wrong. Sometimes it seems they all want to yell at me. Sometimes I wish I covered golf or fishing.

At ground zero during the November 2000 election recount, I developed a muscle spasm in my left eye. By March 2001 I was in the hospital with pneumonia, exhausted after weeks of reporting about hanging and pregnant chads. Speaking of pregnant, I worked 12-hour days as the lead reporter on the William Kennedy Smith rape case - pregnant and stupid enough to miss my last trimester check-ups rather than miss a day in court. I gave birth 10 days after the verdict.

I do not have an off-switch.

Of course if my illnesses could speak, they would tell you that I have the perfect job. Little Miss Bipolar would tell you how exhilarating journalism is - your mind has to race to keep up with what is going on and the constant stream of tension and anger is so invigorating! Mr. Alcoholic would remind you that every good journalist has a bottle in the drawer and every good newspaper has a bar across the street. And my depression would tell you how grateful she is for the endless supply of stress, sleep-deprivation and racing thoughts - washed down with a stiff one after deadline.

I have been committing journalism for so long - almost 30 years - that this lifestyle, pace and drama seem normal to me. I don't respect my stress because I don't recognize it as stress. It's my life. I am used to it. But that does not mean it is right or good. It isn't. I learned that after my last major depression three years ago. Just because a behavior or way of thinking is comfortable does not mean it is healthy. When I learned this it was as though the clouds had parted and I could see what an utter idiot I had been. I had been holding the hand that held me down.

I am still an investigative reporter. I still love my job. My boss still tells me to go home. I still get yelled at. Today I know there is a very, very fine line between loving what you do and letting that love kill you. I can't always see that line and sometimes I just ignore it. But I know that line is there. Some days, that is the best I can do.

The inner vibe of my mania

I have a meeting today. 1 p.m. I had a meeting on the same topic last week. It did not go well.

I do not do well at meetings. Besides having a hard time sitting still, I apparently vibrate. I throw out energy when I get excited about an idea, try to persuade others to accept my ideas or defend my ideas. I can think very quickly on my feet. Throw a question at me and I will drop it into my blender-brain, spin it around at a few thousand rpm and within seconds, a smooth response pours from my mouth.

Apparently, the intensity with which I do this intimidates others - especially those in positions above me who realize that they should have come up with my idea. My therapist pointed this out to me. I could have the best idea in the world but the words I use, the tone of my voice and my intensity turn people off - especially men.

I feel really bad about this. I did not realize I was doing it. I do not want or intend to insult anyone. It's just that sometimes a switch goes off in my brain and I suddenly feel like a racehorse at the gate, one hoof pawing at the dirt. Open the gate and I'm gone. I might win the race but no one wants to play with me. I heard a psychiatrist say last week that throughout history, many great rulers were bipolar.

I am going to work on my inner vibe today. I am going to listen to the tone of my voice, watch my body language and feel the vibe of my mania during this meeting. I have an idea - a really good idea - I want to throw out there. I want others to accept it. Most of all, I do not want to scare or intimidate others with my vibrating brain. We will see how it goes.

My 12-step anti-depression program

Most of us know the thoughts and behaviors of depression. No brainer: sleep or sleeplessness; eat a lot or none at all; racing thoughts; anxiety; desperation; fear; lethargy; disinterest; loneliness and on and on. What takes more effort is to figure out the thoughts and behaviors of the opposite state of mind.

I have given this some thought over the last few years and have come up with a 12-step anti-depression program. The great thing about 12-step programs is that they are programs of suggestions, not requirements.

You may not be able to do these "suggestions" while you are in your black hole, but vow to do at least one when you are back on terra firma. Take what you want and leave the rest. Here we go:

1. Never, ever walk past a slab of wet cement without leaving your mark.

2. Ride a bike.

3. Swing (as in "swing-set" but only if there are no kids waiting for the swing.)

4. Renew your faith in the youth of America. Watch *Rob and Big* on MTV.

5. Go to a high school homecoming football game, even if you do not like football, know nothing about the school, and don't know anyone in the stands.

6. Always keep fudgesicles and popsicles in your freezer. Eat one every night. (They make all this stuff sugar and fat-free now so you have no excuse.)

7. Ride a bike, again.

8. Jump rope. If you are not in good enough shape, twirl.

9. Go to a grocery store in a poor part of town and stick a $20 bill between packages of diapers or formula. Walk away. Tell no one.

10. Scratch a dog on its sweet spot so its back leg goes spastic.

11. Tell a kid that you think you lost a $1 bill under "there" - then point to couch, chair, table, desk, bed, whatever. Tell the kid that he can have it if he can find it. When the kid asks "Under where?" say "HA! MADE YOU SAY UNDERWEAR!" Then reach in your pocket and give the kid a buck.

12. Did I mention ride a bike - preferably to an ice cream store. If you cannot ride a bike, drive to the local ice cream store, sit and have a cone. With sprinkles.

Worrying about depression

My mother - God love her - was a professional worrier.

Brought up in an Irish-Catholic home in a small Wisconsin farm community, it was her way of showing that she loved us. The more you worried - and showed it and said it - the more you love someone. She loved us a lot. She worried constantly. Even when she wasn't saying what she was worried about, you could tell by the look on her face that she was worried about something.

Today, I am trying not to worry. It is not easy. It is in the double-helix of my DNA. I am having a very difficult time right now. On Monday I got word that the results of a routine medical procedure were abnormal. On Tuesday I got word that some routine blood tests showed "mild abnormalities" and I should come in for more tests.

I watched myself turn into my mother - God love her. I became sullen, withdrawn and got that worried mom-look on my face. My mood turned sour. I wanted to be alone. I worried myself into an imaginary surgery, bald head and skin and bones. I projected so far out into my worrisome future that I worked until 8 p.m. last night just to avoid my worry - which got my boss worried about my depression. Then I got worried about my worrying because I know that worrying is NOT good for my depression. It is a trigger. And I worry when my finger is on the trigger.

Then I heard the sweet little voice of my daughter from long ago.

"Mom, what's wrong?" my daughter asked me 10 years ago, when she was just 7.

"I'm worried about…" (something I cannot even remember today.)

"Mom, you know that worrying is a sin," she told me.

"What?" I asked her.

"Worrying shows God that you don't trust him," she said.

Ouch. Out of the mouths of babes. She was right. Worrying is absolutely worthless. It is the opposite of faith - in myself, my friends, my body and my God. Today, when I catch myself worrying I run through my list of worries.

Have I scheduled all the appointments? Yes.

Have I gotten the time off work? Yes.

Have I kept myself in good enough physical condition to confront whatever lies ahead? Absolutely.

Do I have friends who would take care of my daughter and me? Absolutely.

Do I have good medical, disability and nursing care insurance? Absolutely.

Can I financially weather a medical crisis? Absolutely.

The only thing left on my worry list is…my dog, "Dog." He really needs to go to the pond everyday. He needs to chase some squirrels and he needs someone to chase him around the dining room table. He needs someone to peel his string cheese.

If that is the worst thing I have to worry about today, it is going to be a great day. I have nothing to worry about. I am going to trust that God will find someone to peel his string cheese.

Reminiscing about my depression

Yesterday was my anniversary. I am not married and I was not celebrating another year of sobriety.

April 27 is the anniversary of my last clinical depression. It was one of the worst days of my life. That was three years ago - April 27, 2006. I got up sometime between 4 and 5 am. I hadn't slept much. I walked the dog to the park, sat on a picnic table and cried. I just wanted some relief. I slogged down to my gym, got on a stationery bike and rode until I foamed the mouth. Nothing. No endorphins.

I got dressed and went to work. I walked in and felt that I was not in my body. I sat at my desk with my back to the newsroom. I was weary. I could not stitch my thoughts together. I was barely eating or sleeping and smothered by anxiety and desperation. I walked out.

I went home and sent a text to my boss. I couldn't talk to her. I didn't know what to say. I called a friend who has depression. She told me I must see a doctor immediately - or go to a hospital emergency room. I found a nurse practitioner who specializes in working with addicts and alcoholics. She saw me that afternoon - probably saving me from relapse. She started me on antidepressants and a mild antipsychotic to help me sleep.

After six weeks of hell and progress measured in little baby steps I returned to work. I gradually slid back into a new life - A.D. - After Depression. Nothing is the same. I can go weeks now - actually months - on terra firma. No crashes. No blastoffs. It is so amazing. I am still in awe of how stable my life is today - even when things around me fall apart. This is what it must feel like to have a healthy brain.

I used to wonder how long this would last. I don't anymore. This is my new life. If I get sick again I will know what to expect and what to do. There is a floor beneath me now. It has been there since April 27, 2006 - my anniversary.

What time is it? NOW

There could not be a more beautiful morning.

The sun is just barely up - no clouds in the sky. The temperature is perfect - you can sit quietly on a bench without feeling a chill or ride your bike without breaking a sweat. There is a light breeze coming out of the southeast. The palm trees are gently swaying.

But me, I can't stop thinking about that stupid meeting Thursday afternoon and how frustrated I got when my idea - which I have been working on for a month - was shot down as soon as it came out of my mouth. I hate that.

I am stuck back on Thursday, missing this beautiful Sunday morning. I am missing the fact that at this moment in time, everything is wonderful. My dog is trotting the perfect distance in front of my bike without tangling his leash. My teenage daughter is still in bed after spending her Saturday night hanging out with friends in our backyard. I seemed to have lost a couple of pounds when I got on the scale this morning. My bills are paid and I made my last car payment this month. Best of all, I have no hangover - I am sober.

But I am stuck on that damn meeting on Thursday. What is WRONG with me? I have a really hard time being in the now. I am always three days in the past - still at some stupid meeting - or ten years in the future - worried about my 401(k). NOW passes me by.

I know this is bad. It is this kind of stinkin' thinkin' that triggers anxiety, anger and fear - essential ingredients for my depression. I have been working on this for years. I do not know if I have made much progress beyond recognizing that I am doing it. But I keep trying.

My first lesson in NOW began about years ago when I took off my watch. I had a really nice watch - a Cartier given to me for my 20th anniversary of writing for the newspaper. I gave my watch to my daughter. I realized that looking at a watch made me think about where I needed to be in two hours or where I had been six hours ago. Not knowing what time it is forces me to ask, "What time is it?" The answer is always "NOW." Amazingly, I am never late.

This morning I practiced another lesson. I used my senses. I asked myself: What do you hear? Birds, my dog's claws clicking on the sidewalk as he trots in front of my bike, the rustle of wind through the trees.

What do you smell? The jasmine on the fence, and - unfortunately - dog doo. What do you taste? Coffee. What do you feel? The wind on my face, the tug on the leash and the sun on my skin. What do you see? 4 ducks, 1 egret and 1 anhinga drying her wings at the pond - and a very happy dog.

This is why I ride a bike. It is always NOW on my bike. On my bike I can smell the jasmine on the fence, I can feel the wind on my face, I can hear my dog's nails on the pavement and I can see the ducks, egrets and anhinga. I miss all that in a car. I look at the cars whizzing by and I realize they don't see the ducks, egret and anhinga. They don't smell the jasmine or feel the breeze or hear their dog's nails on the sidewalk because their windows are rolled up and they are going too fast.

The road they are on does not take them close enough to the pond to see the birds. Their road does not lead to the swing set where I stop and do a little swingin'. They are going too fast to say "Mornin'" to the other folks walking their dogs or working in their yards. It is not NOW when you are in a car. It is always WHERE and WHEN - "WHERE am I going?" "WHEN will I get there?" I gave my car to my daughter.

And now I am ready to start my day over again. Good mornin'. What time is it?

The antidepressant that lives and loves

Twenty-one polo ponies died here last Sunday.

I do not know much about polo. But I do understand this:

"These horses give you their all," said one of the world's top polo player. "They are like the best dog you ever had."

The best dog I ever had died in my arms. Her death capped a 22 month wave of death that finally pulled me under. My father died first. Sixteen months later, my mother. Eight month after that - my eternally faithful and infinitely loving dog Bella died.

Of the three I cried the hardest when my beautiful Weimeraner Bella died. Maybe it was accumulated grief. But I wept like I had never wept before. I dug a hole in the backyard and buried her. My daughter and I made a headstone from a children's craft kit designed for imprinting little hands in cement.

I replaced Bella several months later with another Weimeraner named Bella - the fourth dog in my life to carry that name. Bella IV is my depression dog. She stayed beside me through my descent to hell and refused to abandon me. She did not judge my illness and she had utter faith I would get better.

I consider her as vital to my recovery as my medications and therapy. When I did not want to get out of bed she reminded me - with those piercing yellow eyes - that she had a bladder and if I did not get my butt out of bed there would be trouble. When I could not sleep she, too, would awaken and accompany me on my sad wanderings through our silent neighborhood.

When I had no love to give, she snuggled beside me and asked for nothing. She watched me. She knew something was wrong. She never left me alone. She waited. Even though I know nothing about polo, I do understand that devastating loss. I understand why grief counselors were brought in for the players, the trainers and the workers who cleaned these ponies' stables.

I know the priceless value of an animal that lives for nothing more than to please and love you, even when you are exhausted and can give nothing back. I know how important it is to have something in my life that gently reminds me that life goes on and that I am needed. I know that I love and need my dog and I will say a prayer today for those grieving the loss of their ponies.

Happiness: The final frontier

When you spend a lifetime trying to make other people happy, you forget what makes you happy. You convince yourself that making other people happy makes you happy. You become so consumed in making others happy - people pleasing - that you have to think - really think - when you are asked what you would like for your birthday.

You come up with gift ideas that you know would make others happy. Slippers. An apron. Perfume. A photo album. Or the ever-popular gift certificate. They are clueless. They don't know what makes you happy because you don't know what makes you happy. You try on the apron, stare at the gift card and try on the slippers.

Secretly, you seethe. Then you go back to making them happy with a huge chip on your shoulder. You try to ignore the resentment but it grows because now they expect you to make them happy. You get angry - with yourself and them. You sit on the pity pot and listen to those tapes in your head that say what you really want to say - You take me for granted! You don't appreciate all I do for you! You expect me to do everything!

That was me. That was the kind of behavior I had to unlearn when I was finally diagnosed with depression and bipolar. The medications were not enough. I had been holding the hand that held me down. This behavior fueled my depression. I had to learn a new way of life.

So, I asked myself "What makes ME happy?" Silence. Hmmm. More silence. Hmmm. Even more silence. Hmmm. What makes ME happy? Took me awhile. SCUBA DIVING! That would make ME really happy. I live a mile from the ocean, on the northern edge of the only reef off the continental U.S.

I did it. I got certified. Every Saturday morning - water temp and weather permitting - I sit on the bow of the dive boat. Then I put on my gear, jump in the ocean and gently fall to the ocean floor. No cell phones, no television, no iPods, no newspapers. Just God and me.

More happiness flowed. A bicycle. I love riding a bike. I gave my daughter my car. Now I commute to work, the grocery store and the beach on my bike. Tap dancing! I tried it. I truly stink. Fishing! I picked up a fly rod and watched the line dance before me. I fell in love.

Once I cracked the shell, happiness flowed. I no longer ask myself - What makes YOU happy. I wait for the inspiration - then I go for it. And right now, I gotta go. The fish are biting.

Codependency: I am She as You are He as You are Me and We are All Together

Where do I end and you begin?

You could be a stranger and I would not know. Your problems are mine. Your consequences are my challenges. "I will take care of that." "You don't have to worry about it." "Lemme see what I can do."

This is my codependency. It is masked in selflessness and martyrdom. "Go ahead. I didn't want it anyway." "Oh, you shouldn't have." "I would never think of…"

I will offer advice and directions when you don't want it. I will push and pull you at the same time. I am like a tick - I will dig my fingernails into your psyche and suck out your free will. No matter what you do to me, you cannot get rid of me. I will mask all my demands in good intentions. I will take care of all your needs — even the ones you do not know you have — and you will feel guilty. I will mirror your feelings.

Nothing I do will ever be good enough. You will embarrass me if you praise me. I will resent you if you don't let me help. I will never ask for anything and I will lavish gifts and favors on you. "Let's do what you want to do." "Why don't we go to your favorite restaurant?" "That's OK. I know you didn't mean it."

Someday I'm gonna make some man a wonderful doormat.

I had heard about codependency. It sounded like psychobabble. Then, on April 27, 2006, I fell into the darkest hole I could have imagined. To get out I needed medicine and a new way of living. Not just eating better and getting more exercise. I needed a new paradigm. I needed to be willing to accept that my good deeds were often bad. My right was wrong. Your free will was not mine. And God forbid - I deserved more.

I went to codependency camp at a treatment center. The cost was about $3,000 (including airfare) and I had never spent that much money on myself. I cringed with guilt. I was scared. It was excruciating but thrilling work. It was as if the clouds had parted and I could see what a complete #$%&@^ I had been. I could also see that I deserved more - like those red, patent leather, pointy-toed stilettos at Nordstrom and maybe even a manicure! Wow.

Three years later I am still working on my codependency. I will never stop. But today I recognize my codependency. I stop those old behaviors before they get out of hand. I ask my friends to help me. I keep the red, patent leather, pointy-toed stilettos in a box on a shelf in my closet. Sometimes I wear them for no reason at all. I deserve it.

Monday, Monotony and Depression

Monday. 7 am. Time to jump back into the gerbil wheel.

Sometimes it is the eternal monotony of doing the next right thing, putting one foot in front of the other that kills me. I am not tired. I am weary.

Walk the dog. Read the paper. Take a shower. Ride to work. Make the car payment. Schedule a mammogram. Write, write, write. Work, work, work. Meeting. Write, write, write. Work, work, work. Lunch. Write, write, write. Work, work, work. Appointment. Write, write, write. Work, work, work. Cook dinner. And on and on and on. Wah, wah, wah.

"Would you like a glass for your whine, madam?"

This is the kind of thinking that can fuel dysthemia, a low-grade depression that is durable, dependable and enduring - great traits for a car - not a life. When you have dysthemia, everyday is Monday. The sky is always March-in-Michigan gray. Dysthemia goes on and on and on - like your mortgage payment. It is not like a major clinical depression. It is a white noise kind of depression. You get so used to it that you are not aware of it. It's just the way life is. Right?

Wrong. I am not powerless. I can take my medications, pray and compile a mental gratitude list. Here is my list:

Yea, the dog is a pain in the butt but he does not chew or snack on the contents of the wastebasket. He is a good watchdog. Yea, he drinks from the toilet - but he never leaves the seat up.

Yea, work is work - BUT YOU HAVE A JOB!!!

Yea, scheduling all these doctor and dentist appointments is a hassle - BUT YOU HAVE MEDICAL INSURANCE!!!

Yea, cooking dinner is a drag - BUT YOU HAVE FOOD, A KITCHEN AND A GREAT LITTLE HOUSE.

I read somewhere that if you have depression, constant thoughts of bad can program the brain to think more bad thoughts. We instinctively cop to the negative. Our proverbial cup is always half empty. But just like I exercise my body, I can exercise my brain. I can compile a gratitude list. I can become aware of the drone of my negative thinking and counter it with gratitude.

A gratitude list is not going to pull me out of the major depression. But a gratitude list raises my awareness of my mental illnesses - depression, bipolar and alcoholism - and reminds me that I am not powerless. I am not a victim.

I am sick. I am taking care of myself.

Unlearned lessons

Alcohol is a depressant. I wished someone had told me this when I was 14, when my drinking career began. Although at that age it wouldn't have meant anything to me. I was going to drink regardless of any warnings.

I drank despite two car accidents and two suicide attempts. I drank to be a part of and I drank to be different. I drank for any good or bad reason or none at all. I only learned three years ago that alcohol is to depression what gasoline is to fire. I am 50.

I knew early on that not drinking made me calmer, more stable and balanced. I actually quit drinking for 10 years, between ages 20-30. Of course I embarked upon a marijuana maintenance plan so I was not exactly clean and sober. I picked up drinking again when I was 30, right where I left off. I was back on the roller coaster.

Ten years, two divorces and one child later, I threw in the towel. I had had enough. I have been sober now for over 10 years. Still, I did not make the connection between alcohol and depression until I was seven years sober. A major depression struck and I had no way to numb the pain. Alcohol was not an option. Asking for help was all I had left.

It worked. Therapy, medications and humility. Today I am healthy. I can look back over the decades and my life makes sense. I do not use my dual-diagnosis as an excuse for things I have done. I use it to stop beating myself up and start making amends. I use it to help me understand myself.

Drinking on my depression explains why, for so many years, I would wake up in the middle of the night and hear a voice in my head, saying to someone: "Oh, she killed herself. She put a gun in her mouth…" It explains why I reached for the drink in the first place - to give me some relief - even a few hours - from my depression. It explains why my hangovers lasted more than a day, because the alcohol in my brain short-circuited synapses that did not work properly because of my depression.

Which came first - the depression or the alcoholism? It does not matter to me. I am definitely an alcoholic. I definitely have depression and bipolar. All that matters is that alcohol is a depressant and I have depression.

Don't should-on me!

I do not like to be "should" on.

If you say "you should" or "you should not" I will seriously consider - maybe even do - the opposite. Maybe it is a symptom of alcoholism or bipolar. Maybe I am just a jerk. I don't know.

The only thing worse than being "should on" is a "Do NOT". If you throw down that verbal gauntlet I will raise an eyebrow and give you that "Oh-Really?" look. Except my nurse practitioner. Her "do NOTS" are holy, like a "Thou Shalt Not."

But I, my friends, am a sinner. For some stupid reason I tinkered with my meds and I am still doing penance. It happened at the end of January. My nurse practitioner told me I could stop taking a medication she had prescribed to help get me through the holidays.

"You should stay on the other medications," she said. Well, Dr. Christine thought it would be OK to drop the dosage of another med she had upped during the holidays. Hey, the holidays are over. Why not just return to my pre-holiday dosages? So, I did it.

Of course I did not tell my nurse practitioner or my therapist or anyone, for that matter. I kept it a secret. About two weeks later I hopped on the roller coaster. Up, up, up I climbed, then dove to the bottom. Up, up, up I climbed, then down to the bottom.

My therapist saw the mania and said I SHOULD call my nurse practitioner. Did I? Of course not. Two weeks later she asked if I had called my nurse practitioner. Of course not. Two weeks later she asked if I had called my nurse practitioner. Of course not. Finally, to get my therapist off my back, I called my nurse practitioner - after hours. I left a message.

My nurse practitioner called back and I confessed. She gently, but firmly told me "DO NOT mess around with your medications!" I realized she was right. I was manic. She told me she had patients who had done what I had done and she was never able to stabilize them again. Bipolar is serious. We love the bipolar-high. "But what goes up WILL come down," she said.

She upped my medications. The mania is leveling. I learned my lesson. I am as sick as my secrets. I need to listen and take directions. Now and forever. Amen.

Give me a Sharpie, a baseball bat and a good pair of boots

Apparently, while in the stupor of my last depression, I was angry. It was hard to believe because all I wanted to do was sleep and wander around the house. But both my therapist and my nurse practitioner told me I was angry and would not get well until I got rid of the anger. I did not know how to do this. In my family we did not get angry. We seethed. We cut people out of our lives, avoided them and refused to make eye contact. We kept our anger inside. Good girls don't get angry.

So, when I learned that anger turned inward was fueling my depression, I did not know what to do. My therapist handed me a whiffle bat and wanted me to whiffle a stuffed animal in her office. A whiffle bat? I am not a whiffle bat kind of girl, I told her. I went home and used a real bat on a pillow. It felt good. I realized that I was angry - real angry - and that pounding pillows was not going to do it for me. I needed to beat the *#%! out of something. I needed to break something, hear the power of my anger and feel it.

I opened the Yellow Pages and found a junkyard. I grabbed a Sharpie, my bat, steel-toed boots and a Rolling Stones CD. It was raining when I got to the junkyard. I walked up to the counter and explained my predicament. The man agreed and pointed to the corner. "You want a bat?"

"No," I explained, "I have my own." A nice metal bat.

The man walked me to a smashed up truck. "This is the only one you can hit," he said. "You gonna scream?"

"I don't know," I said. He walked away. I surveyed the truck, walked around to the hood and took out my Sharpie. I wrote the names of all the people I believed had wronged me. Then I went at it. I have no idea how long I was there. Over and over and over I raised up that bat and slammed it down. I broke windows, smashed headlights, kicked side panels and pounded on that hood until I was shaking and breathless. Then I went at it some more.

When it was over I walked back to the office and asked the man if he wanted me to clean up my mess. He said "No." I drove home listening to The Rolling Stones, full blast. Then I collapsed. I do not recommend this kind of anger-management. I am a very athletic woman but for days my body ached. Rage and adrenalin.

My therapist was not pleased. I should not have done this alone, she said. Pent up rage is dangerous and uncontrollable. We can end up hurting ourselves if we go at it alone, she said. She taught me how to deal with my anger in healthy ways. Pause when agitated. Prevent an argument from getting out of hand with "We need to agree to disagree." Put my face in a pillow and yell. Find a road with little traffic, roll up the windows and scream. And for God sake, use a whiffle bat next time.

Anger is difficult for women. We are taught that good girls do not get into arguments and do not raise their voices. We do not rough house. We do not have sports like football and hockey that allow us to hit and tackle. The best we can do is smack a tennis ball with all our might. We are so unaccustomed to anger and bury it so deep that we do not recognize it in ourselves. We turn our anger inward. Our anger fuels our depression.

I know the power of my anger. I know it can kill me. I know what it feels like and what to do with it. I put on my bathing suit, do a cannon ball into the pool and scream my lungs out underwater. Then I catch some rays.

Thank God

One of the few good things about being in a deep, dark clinical depression is that it opens your mind. Wide open. Desperation and hopelessness will do that. It did for me. I found a God I could trust.

I was raised an Irish-Catholic - no meat on Fridays, no chocolate during Lent and trading holy cards like baseball cards. Soon as I was old enough I fell away from the church. For decades I bounced back and forth - being an atheist, then an agnostic. It just seemed God never answered my foxhole prayers. Go figure.

When you are in enough pain, you will try anything. The medicine didn't seem to be working. My therapy was at a standstill. Even exercise failed me. What the hell? Why not try God again? What seemed like more unanswered foxhole prayers turned into anger at God, pleading and bargaining with God. Without realizing it I was developing a relationship with a God I had never known.

It finally came down to faith - faith that the medicine would work, faith that I would eventually come out of my black hole, faith that I could handle this, faith that something greater than myself could restore me to sanity. The choice was mine: take off my cape and surrender to faith or go back to wondering if my Prius could produce enough carbon monoxide to kill me. I surrendered to faith.

My foxhole prayers were finally answered. I have a God in my life. She has a wicked sense of humor. He lets me rant at him. It shows itself in the corals and fish I see when I go diving to the bottom of the ocean. We have a pretty good time.

Me, my daughter and Sylvia Plath

Nicholas Hughes, 47, hanged himself last week. Forty-six years ago Hughes' mother, poet Sylvia Plath, placed her head in an oven and turned the gas on while her 2-year-old daughter and one-year-old, Nicholas, Years later Nicholas' stepmother killed herself the same way.

Plath's book, *The Bell Jar*, had a profound affect on me. I had never before identified with a fictional character and I became enamored with Plath. In a sick way, she was my hero. I was 16. In hindsight I should not have read that book when I did. I was too young and too sick. Her depression made her feel as though she was trapped under a bell jar, unable to breathe. Finally, someone felt just like me.

Suicide is not hereditary - at least geneticists have not proved it. However, studies have shown that children whose mothers committed suicide are 7 times more likely to attempt suicide than children whose mothers do not. That statistic is why I am alive. I was suicidal during my last depression. I had tried to kill myself twice before.

My therapist and nurse practitioner told me that statistic. They asked me to remember it when I had suicidal thoughts. It worked. I could never do that to my daughter. Regardless of how I feel about my own life, I love my daughter more than I imagined I could ever love another person. I would never put her life at risk - ever. Today she is 17. She is happy. She just found a dress for her school's Junior-Senior Dinner. We are looking at colleges. She framed a picture of us and gave it to me for Christmas.

She is my anchor to life. I am so blessed to be alive. I have a life I never dreamed of and I am finally the mother I always wanted to be. Don't quit before the miracle.

A healthy addiction? Not for me

Here is my problem with exercise: I am addicted.

My "food issues" love exercise because I can eat more without gaining weight. My mania loves exercise because exercise is - well - manic. My alcoholism loves exercise because you can't be a drunk if you can run that far and fast before 6 a.m. Even my depression loves exercise because the sports I like - swimming, cycling, running, weight training - I do alone.

I have promised my therapist that I will not exercise more than four times a week (scuba diving does not count. It's just floating). But it's not easy when everyone around you says, "Well, if you gotta have an addiction it might as well be exercise" or "Boy, I wish I had that addiction" or "At least you have a healthy addiction."

What is a healthy addiction?

It has been nearly 11 years since I had a drink or a drug but I still struggle with my exercise addiction. Actually, I'm lying. I don't struggle with my exercise addiction. My therapist struggles with my exercise addiction. That's the problem. Despite years of sobriety, my addict brain can still convince me that this addiction is better than that addiction. Sure, I look a heckuva lot better than a crack addict, but we are both addicts. Any addiction - to drugs, alcohol, food or behaviors - is toxic to me, my depression and bipolar.

I can easily - and have - been addicted to my work. If I am not careful, I could become addicted to that TV show *House*. Why am I torqued about this right now? Because every night about this time - 9:30 - I start thinking about tomorrow's workout. If it is Wednesday night I start planning for Thursday 7 a.m. boot camp. Some people decide what they are going to wear tomorrow. I decide what I am going to work out - abs, glutes, biceps..."

I like to think that today I have a handle on my exercise addiction. Back in the days when I did triathlon and ran marathons I worked out six, sometimes seven days a week. Sometimes twice a day. I spent outrageous sums of money on bikes and shoes and a ridiculous amount of time training. Just like a meth addict, I surrounded myself with other exercise addicts. Except we were the healthy addicts. Yea, right.

Despite sitting here writing this right now, I AM going to the 7 a.m. boot camp tomorrow. It will be my third workout this week - so I still have one left for Friday. I will just have to make it through the weekend without any. Oh man, it's a holiday weekend - a three-day weekend! You can't expect me to go the whole weekend without any. Just a little, just to have some fun on the weekend, won't hurt. Just so long as I don't do too much...

Sound familiar?

Guilt, shame and depression

Today is the second straight day I woke up with this feeling - no, it's deeper than a feeling - that I had done something wrong.

Back in the days before I was diagnosed with depression and before I quit drinking, I woke with this feeling - sensation - every morning. Every single morning. A heaviness in my chest. My mind racing to find a wrong and them chomp onto it like a pit bull.

Often, there was a wrong. I drank too much the night before. I was a rotten mom. I had lost it with a public official I was interviewing for a story. If I could not find a wrong, I threw the back of my hand to my brow and indulged my impending martyrdom: my husband (now ex-) neglected, disrespected and ignored me; it's sooooo hard being a working mom; must I do everything around here?

And if that didn't explain the feeling in my chest, I could nibble on a resentment that marinated overnight: Will you look at those rich, thin, beautiful women? They are so ignorant and vapid!; Of course I would rather be home in an apron, baking chocolate chip cookies and watching Oprah but some of us women HAVE to work; Oh, great: They promoted another white guy.

This is what the brain of a dysthemia alcoholic sounds like. Constantly searching for the bad in every person and situation. Fuel for a miserable life and major depression. Then I quit drinking, began therapy and started taking antidepressants and mood stabilizers.

The clouds parted. I learned to identify rather than compare. I was taught how to stay on my side of the street and to make an amends. But the most important lesson I learned was the difference between guilt and shame: Guilt is the feeling that comes from having done something bad; Shame is the belief that you are inherently bad.

Guilt and shame were so tightly intertwined in my psyche that I often could not distinguish one from another. Did I do something bad or do I think I am bad? Hmmmmm. If I had done something bad I need to apologize. If I believe I am bad, I need to turn off that soundtrack. I am not bad. I am not bad. I am not bad...

So, as I lay in bed this morning with "Dog" imbedded in my side, I rewound the security camera's tape from yesterday. I say a prayer and ask: Did I do something bad? Anything? Besides not trimming the hedges, no. I had not.

Which leaves me asking the question: Am I bad? No. I am not. This feeling my chest this morning is shame. Shame is just a feeling - not a fact. I am a good person. I deserve to be happy. I am not bad.

I am going to the park with "Dog."

My depression is rusty

"Heeeeeere comes Rusty!"

That's the announcer at the local kennel club when a race starts. Rusty is steel rabbit on an electric track just above and in front of the greyhounds that zips ahead of the muzzled pack. The dogs don't know why they chase Rusty. They just do.

I don't know why I chase Rusty. I just do. Rusty can be anything in my life: A drink, a man, a raise, a flat tummy. Chasing Rusty is not good. I sprint through my life - wild eyed and out of breath - chasing Rusty. I got to thinking about Rusty this morning.

I joined a group of triathletes at the beach early this morning. I have been a competitive swimmer since I was 7 years old. I gave it up years ago and haven't swum a lap in a couple of years. But I went to the beach this morning telling myself it was time to get back into the water - just a nice leisurely swim.

Damn, out popped Rusty - the lead swimmer was a guy at least 10 years younger than me. No matter, I had to chase. I couldn't go for a leisurely swim as the sun rose over the Atlantic Ocean. I had to chase. What am I chasing? Why am I chasing?

I came home from the beach and took "Dog" to the pond - our morning routine. Dog runs in front of my bike, taking minor detours to chase a squirrel up a tree. There are a lot of squirrels at the pond and they have always run faster than "Dog". Until today. "Dog" finally caught a squirrel. I turned around and watched his head thrashing back and forth with a mouth full of fur. By the time I got to him the squirrel was dead. "Dog" just stood there not knowing what to do. He chased the squirrel. He caught the squirrel. Now what?

Exactly. When you are bipolar you don't ask "why?" You just go. You don't need a reason anymore than the greyhounds need a reason to chase Rusty. You just go. If you are also an alcoholic - dual diagnosed - you don't ask why you need to drink. You just drink. It is the way life is. You go, and then you drink. You go, and then you drink...

God help you if you ever catch and kill Rusty. Unlike "Dog", who shrugs his little dog shoulders and trots off looking for another squirrel, it is not so easy for us bipolar humans. When you have killed enough squirrels, you finally ask, "My God, what have I done?" Then you swan dive into a bottomless black hole of guilt, disgust, remorse and self-loathing and pour yourself a drink or three or nine.

I thought I had gotten rid of the Rustys in my life. With all the therapy, sobriety, medications, prayers, healthy eating and sound sleeping I thought Rusty was gone for good. Until this morning, as I chased down the young guy swimming in front of me. I missed a school of fish and a bikini on the bottom that the swimmers, who know how to enjoy a morning swim, caught sight of.

At least today I can see myself chasing Rusty. I know when I am chasing. I guess that's progress, right? Being aware of this feeling and energy. So, I am making progress, right? They say awareness is the first step to changing a behavior or character defect. Today, I am definitely aware. Very aware.

My picker is broken

Obviously, I choose men who are not exactly compatible and then I stay with them beyond the expiration date. It has taken 50 years, two marriages and a string of unpleasant break-ups to figure this out. Obviously, I am not a quick study.

I am begrudgingly venturing back into the dating game. It ain't pretty. Besides the gray hair, stretch marks and wrinkles there is the matter of my mental illnesses. Plural. How many dates before I throw THAT on the table? "Did I mention that I have depression and bipolar?" "Why don't I drink? Well, I am an alcoholic." Let me throw menopause on the menu, too. And THE BLACK PLAGUE.

Am I a catch or what?

What's a guy supposed to say to all of that? Then there is the matter of the medications...and therapy...and meetings. "But hey, if you want to know that stuff about me, you can read my column that's published in newspapers throughout North America or my web site or my blog. Don't worry, everyone knows I am mentally ill. Besides, I don't write about the guys I date anymore. I learned THAT lesson."

Excuse me, I have a line of white knights at my front door.

Seriously, what's a mentally ill, menopausal, addicted woman to do? It's not like I can go to a nightclub and get wasted and dance on the bar. I know I'm a bubble off plumb. I know I color outside the lines. Do I look for a guy who is the same? Honestly, I have never been attracted to a guy who is not like me - except for the teeny tiny fact that they are not sober or don't want to admit they are depressed. How am I supposed to turn off that switch? Experience has shown me that if I am attracted to a guy he is probably not compatible with or good for me.

How about online matchmaking! Beyond the fact that my teenage daughter says she will divorce me if I stoop to internet dating, there is the teeny tiny fact of filling out the questionnaire - honestly.

I don't know. It's too overwhelming at this hour of the morning. I'm going to walk the dog. Maybe Mr. Right is at the dog park.

Bipolar: Thinking it through

Among the tools I have been given in recovery is this gem: "Think it through."

Yea, that ice cold, sweaty bottle of Corona with a lime it in looks sooooo good. But what happens after that first sip? You have another. And another, and another, and another.... Then I will do or say something I will regret or I will have no memory of what I did. The next time I see these people I will have to wonder what I said or did to them after I drank 10 Coronas. In the morning I will wake up feeling like #$&*%. My head will be in a vice, my face will be blotchy and my eyes red. I will feel guilty. I will hate myself. I will get depressed.

That is how "thinking it through" works. This is how I stay sober and stable. But "thinking it through" is an unnatural act if you have bipolar, like me. When you are bipolar you think about as far ahead as the next blink of your eye. All kinds of stuff comes out of my mouth. Sometimes I sound almost brilliant and I have to look around to see if someone else said that. Sometimes I say stuff that is amazingly sarcastic and hurtful: "Did I just say that?"

This week I wanted to make a phone call to a guy I used to date. I told my best friend and she helped me think it through: "You know he's not going to answer." "You know you will leave a message and he won't call you back." "You know you will spend the next week checking your cell phone every ten minutes to see if he called or sent a txt." "You know you will drive yourself crazy."

Thank God for best friends. I won't make that call today.

Depression, vacations and carrots

Among the many things my father was told when he was diagnosed with lung cancer was this: Find something to look forward to. He did. Amid his chemo and radiation, I gave birth to his first grandchild. My brother gave him his second and third. My sister his fourth and fifth.

When my mother was diagnosed with cancer, she did the same. Amid her surgery, chemo and radiation there were birthdays and First Communions. Vacations. Christmas. Tea parties. Cookies to be made and books to be read.

I am thinking of my mother and father today and how well they were able to find a carrot and dangle it in front of themselves. Mentally, it kept them strong and fit during their suffering and deaths. It made us feel as though we were as vital to their treatment as their medications. It distracted all of us and gave us hope.

For the last week I have been praying and searching for a carrot. Please God, help me find a carrot today. I am sure there are carrots all around me but I cannot see them. My depression is blinding me. This is how it starts. A dash of dysthemia. A dollop of despair.

I have two weeks vacation coming up. I have nothing planned. Vacations have always been my salvation. I spend months focusing on where I will go, what I will see, who I will travel with, what I will take, what book will I read and on and on. I love to travel. Last summer I went to northern Michigan with a man I was seeing. (Emphasis on "WAS").

This year there is no vacation planned. Maybe that is a good thing. Maybe that is what I need. But I feel so empty. I almost dread taking two-weeks off. I caught myself saying to someone last week: "I have to take two weeks off next month..." I know for my mental health I must get out of here. I need to be away. I want to get away. But where? With whom?

I know I have so much to be grateful for: I have a job, medical benefits, friends and a great dog. My daughter is starting her senior year in high school and we are on the hunt for a college - a milestone that thrills and terrifies me.

But today I need a carrot. I really need a carrot. I need to feel and believe there is something really good just ahead. Something, some place, someone just ahead. Please God, help me find a carrot today.

Depression and the recession

Two days ago we had a meeting at the office. We have learned that when there is a meeting, something big is happening. Little things come in emails. Big things come in meetings. Last summer half the newsroom accepted buyouts after a meeting. Those of us who stayed gathered at 1:30 p.m. on Tuesday.

First, the good news: looks like we have already hit bottom and are on our way up. Then, the wonk news - a new org chart. Forty-five minutes into the presentation of the new org chart came THE NEWS: There will be more layoffs. We don't know when or how many, but sometime before the end of the year. WHAT!!!!

The new org chart became a blur. I couldn't hear what the boss was saying about who will report to whom. I did hear the part about some folks having to re-apply for their jobs. I definitely heard - over and over - the phrase "we will be smaller".

After the meeting I went back to work. I told myself, "You have been through this before. Last summer. You made it. Remember, we decided then that whatever happens, you WILL by OK. You did all your worrying last year. Whatever happens, you will be OK. You will be OK. You will be OK. Onward!"

Wrong.

Last night I had a horrible dream. I was laid off. Twenty-four years with this company, a single-mom with depression and a daughter headed to college next year and I was laid off, escorted from my office immediately. No good-byes. No chance to ask "why me?" Just a door. I dreamed I was not allowed in the building. I was an outcast.

Apparently, I did not do all my worrying last summer. This summer, too, will be a summer of uncertainty. Anxiety, fear and worry. Bad dreams and frenetic workdays - if I just work harder and faster they won't lay me off. If ever there was a prescription FOR depression, this is it.

I have to pull out my toolbox again. Eat right, exercise, pray, see the therapist, call your girlfriends, pray some more, take your meds, count your blessings not the dollars in your 401(k). Breathe. I got through this once without diving into my black hole. I can do it again.

Right?

Essential silly

When my mother's cancer metastasized I bought a plastic sumo wrestler for my dashboard. It jiggled like a bobble-head doll, and I could get him to wag like a dog's tail by making a sharp turn. It was silly and I needed silly.

Mr. Sumo did not keep me from falling into a deep depression after my mother's death. But he helped me learn the value of silly and the depth of the love between a mother and her daughter. My mother was not an especially happy woman. I remember her as frustrated, overworked, worried and weary. I loved her very much and wanted her to be happy.

When I was little I tried very hard to make her happy. Good report cards, blue ribbons and staying between the lines. When I was 14 my mental illnesses took a hold of me, and I became a rebellious she-cat in a monogrammed sweater. My mother and I were enemies for years. It took me 40 years to realize I was not responsible for her happiness and that we probably shared the same mental illness - a low-grade, long-lasting depression called dysthemia.

In her final years she embraced silly. Those are the memories I choose to remember. She made buckets of homemade bubble mix and created a wand that made huge bubbles for her grandkids. She made Mr. Bubble beards on the kids in the bathtub and created a stage in the basement with an old sheet hanging from a clothesline.

It took me years after her death to learn about silly. Depression is a very serious illness, and we become very, very serious people. Everything is serious when you are depressed. Walking the dog, washing your hair or watching a pot of water boil. Very serious stuff. Depression leaves no room for silly.

My poor daughter missed out on a lot of silly when I was depressed. I feel bad about that. It is horrible for a child to believe that she is responsible for her mother's happiness or unhappiness. The child of a mentally ill parent must constantly be reminded that she is not responsible for that, or for the sickness that makes their mom unhappy.

Today, silly is an essential skill in my mothering repertoire - even though it often embarrasses my 17-year-old daughter. I will seek new ways to make the dog chase his tail. I will continue to make animal-shaped pancakes that all look like snakes or fat dogs. I will always rearrange the silver N-O-E-L letters on the Christmas mantel to read L-E-O-N. It is the least I can do.

Jumbled thoughts

U-S-V-E-A

I am trying to unscramble these letters. It is supposed to "form an ordinary word," according to the Jumble instructions in the paper. I have been at it for a while now, an embarrassing while now, considering I am a writer.

This is a new tool to help me stop - or at least divert - the "stinkin' thinkin'" that can start when I am in a funk. And I am in a funk. When this happens I obsess over the person, place, thing or situation that triggered the funk. I don't talk about it. I let it wreak havoc in my head. I give it my undivided attention. After a few days it seeps into my subconscious and I start dreaming about it. Then I notice the muscles in my face have gone slack and I am very, very tired.

I am on an emotional luge and I have to stop before I pick up any more speed. Hence, the Jumble. A good friend told me she does the Jumble every morning. She said it is good exercise for her brain. I'm not sure my brain needs any more exercise but it certainly needs direction and self-restraint, like that Weimaraner I used to own.

I learned about the concept of mind training from the Dalai Lama and a friend old enough to remember record players. In Tibetan Buddhism the concept of training, disciplining, and calming the mind is called Lojong. The practice involves focusing your thoughts and actions on dozens of proverbs to correct bad mental habits that cause anxiety, fear, anger and other fuels for depression. Frankly, I suck at it.

I prefer to use my friend's Western thought control technique. Say you are listening to an album on a record player and a song you really dislike - such as anything by Tony Orlando and Dawn - comes on. You pick up the arm, stop the annoying music, and move it to a song that you really like. When my obsessive, negative thoughts take over, visualize picking up the arm and placing it on a thought you really like - such as anything that involves a hammock.

When these techniques do not work, I need a task that demands intense focus. I am blessed to have a career that requires intense focus. But there are days - like today - when I need to have one of those tasks waiting for me as soon as I roll out of bed.

Jumble.

It is noon and I still have not figured out U-S-V-E-A. I also have not spent the entire morning consumed with depression-provoking, obsessive thoughts. The beautiful thing is that when I unscramble U-S-V-E-A there are three more Jumbles!

Weight, food, body image and depression

It's the least wonderful time of the year: The resurrection of last year's bathing suit.

I dread this. Weight and age issues play a huge role in managing my bipolar and depression. Gaining as little as 2 or 3 pounds can trigger a manic episode of emotional self-flagellation and obsessive exercise. I don't care about my hair going gray (or "silver" as I choose to call it) but those wagging water balloons dangling from my triceps and dough rolling over the top of my jeans make me sad.

According to body-mass index charts, I am smack in the middle of the normal range for a woman of my height. Still, I won't eat wheat or pop so much as one M&M.

Those who know me are probably rolling their eyes at what appears to be vanity. But this obsession with my weight is one of a smorgasbord of mental illness side dishes that complement the main course - depression and bipolar.

Many, many women with overeating, under-eating and body image disorders suffer from undiagnosed depression and bipolar. And many women with depression and bipolar also suffer from undiagnosed eating and body-image disorders. My therapist and psych-nurse practitioner understood this, screened me for these other disorders and discovered my obsession with the scale.

Not all women are as lucky. Operators of weight-loss programs and clinics are not trained to screen for depression. And there are doctors who prescribe antidepressants to women who have been frighteningly enhanced with multiple plastic surgeries without screening them for body image disorders. Who knows whether the depression is symptom of an eating or body-image disorder or the disorder is a symptom of the depression? Or maybe both.

Perhaps the problem is that we view eating and body-image disorders as entertainment rather than mental illnesses. We want before and after photos of the celeb who gained 50 pounds. We watch television programs that award $250,000 to obese contestants who lose the most weight. We shake our heads at a photo timeline of Michael Jackson's nose.

Maybe somewhere over the rainbow plastic surgeons will be required to screen patients for body-image disorders and family physicians will look for food addictions before prescribing antidepressants. As for me, I know I have depression and weight issues. It doesn't matter which one came first, I know I have to treat them both.

As for last year's bathing suit, I can't seem to find mine. Apparently I lost it. I take this as a sign: Forget about it. Just buy a damn bathing suit and wear your life like a comfy, loose-fitting, lightweight beach cover-up.

Admit, accept and own it

Ad♦mit (ad mit') 1. To permit to enter or use; let in.

147

Ac•cept (ak sept') 1. To take (what is offered or given); receive, esp. willingly.

It took me a long time to figure out the difference between admitting I have a problem and accepting the problem.

For many years I knew that my "ups" were too up and my "lows" were too low. I knew I had a "drinking problem." I had no problem admitting these problems - to myself. I believed that admitting a problem was enough. I was being honest, right? I was not hiding anything. I was not in denial. I was just acknowledging reality.

But my life was not getting better. I could not figure out why.

It got to the point where the more problems I admitted to, the worse things became. I admitted that I had become estranged from my brother and sister. I admitted - with a megaphone - that the single-working mom thing left me with no time for myself. I admitted my dog was driving me crazy. I admitted I was overworked and underpaid. I admitted that my marriage was in trouble. I admitted it was all my husband's fault. To me, admitting a problem was the same as accepting a problem.

Au contraire. There is a big difference. I do not remember who taught me the difference, but the clouds parted, I grimaced and understood why I was miserable and why my depression would not lift.

I had heard about acceptance, read about it and thought it was a dandy idea: "Let go and let God." "Turn it over." "Accept your admission." Yada, yada, yada. I was clueless about what acceptance meant or how to do it.

I learned. Whether it is a dog or a disease, accepting a problem means I own it. It is my problem, not yours. It means I am responsible for finding a solution.

I did not like this. It did not seem fair. It sounded like a lot of work.

When I accepted that my "ups" were too up and my "lows" were too low, I asked for help and learned I have depression and bipolar. I accepted that I need therapy and medication to get better. When I accepted my "drinking problem," I accepted that I am an alcoholic and quit drinking. I got in touch with my brother and sister. I stopped wearing a watch. I gave away the dog. I stopped blaming my husband and looked at my side of the street. I got divorced.

I got better. I got a life

Forgive us our illnesses

In 1957, the American Medical Association accepted alcoholism as an illness. At about the same time, alcoholism found a place in the American Psychiatric Association's Diagnostic and Statistical Manual - the hallowed handbook that doctors use to diagnose mental illness (and that insurance companies use to deny your claim).

In other words, alcoholism is an illness. It is a mental illness. People who have alcoholism, like me, are not weak or lacking discipline. In fact, most of the alcoholics I know - in recovery and still drinking - are very strong and very disciplined. That's how we convince ourselves that we are in control and what makes us so annoying.

Learning that alcoholism is a legitimate illness helped me immensely. It gave me some self-esteem, hope and the final word in conversations with know-it-alls who believe we could quit drinking if we really, really tried: "Well I guess you know more than the American Medical Association because the AMA decided that alcoholism is an illness 50 years ago."

Depression is different. There are a lot of people who admit that depression is a real illness. They feign sympathy and tell you about someone else's struggle with depression. But you can tell by their zealous enthusiasm that they don't really believe it. I hate to admit this: I was among them.

I knew that Hippocrates declared depression a real illness several thousand years before the American Psychiatric Association. Folks that I admired - Michelangelo, Eric Clapton and Tony Dow, the guy who played Beaver's brother, Wally - all suffered from depression. But when dealing with someone with depression, I privately thought: "Get a grip already, will ya?"

When I was diagnosed with a depression - a major clinical depression - what helped me more than the manuals and medical endorsements were the aw-shucks comments from friends: "I've been on antidepressants for years." Or, "Actually, I am on two antidepressants." Or, "I have to be on either antidepressants or hormones or I'm a mess."

Really? Who would have guessed?

The moral is simple: Do whatever it takes to accept and forgive yourself for being mentally ill.

Made in the USA
San Bernardino, CA
26 December 2015